Mentoring and Coaching

Articles from HUMAN CAPITAL REVIEW

http://www.humancapitalreview.org

Edited by Johan Herholdt

kr
publishing

2012

First published in 2012

ISBN: 978-1-86922-182-9

Published by Knowres Publishing (Pty) Ltd
Republic of South Africa

Tel: (+27 11) 706 6009
E-mail: orders@knowres.co.za
Website: www.kr.co.za

Typesetting, layout and design: Replika Press Pvt Ltd, Haryana, India
Cover design: Sean Sequeira, idDigital, sean@iddigital.co.za
First editing and proofreading: Nicky Neville. nickyn@bulembu.org
Second editing and proofreading: Adrienne Pretorius, pretorii@mweb.co.za
Project management: Cia Joubert, cia@knowres.co.za

ACKNOWLEDGEMENTS

Special thanks to **Michele Butler-van Eeden,** *Editor: Human Capital Review*, which is Knowledge Resources' online magazine (www. humancapitalreview.org), for all her tireless work in searching for and packaging these articles on a monthly basis.

Special thanks to all the contributors who generously share their knowledge with us. We value these contributions from industry professionals and leaders, who have also made it possible to publish a new series – the *Human Capital Review* series.

ABOUT HUMAN CAPITAL REVIEW ONLINE MAGAZINE

⦿ HUMAN CAPITAL REVIEW

Human Capital Review is a monthly online magazine serving the human resources and human resources development fraternities in Africa. It features interesting and informative content from internationally renowned authors and professionals from leading organisations who have made a significant contribution to the development of human capital.

The magazine provides readers with valuable information, which:

- Serves as a practical, informative resource, covering the latest thinking, trends, challenges, and solutions within the human capital arena, throughout established and emerging nations

- Provides HR professionals with a resource to assist them in contributing to the development of their profession.

Human Capital Review offers authoritative and strategic articles which provide fresh and original viewpoints and practical solutions, resulting in enhanced performance. The focus is on both national and international perspectives, with specific implications for practitioners in emerging markets.

This useful online magazine is presented in a high-quality format and includes articles on both fundamental and topical processes, programmes and policies; case studies illustrating practical application of human resources theory and good practice; surveys; interviews; checklists; tools; highly recommended books; and information on training conferences, seminars, and workshops.

Specific topics include assessment; corporate social investment; diversity and equity; good governance; human capital management; HR development; HR strategy; industrial relations; labour issues; leadership; performance management; remuneration; talent management; team development; transformation; and many more.

With a readership that is growing on a daily basis, *Human Capital Review* is currently (September 2011) read by more than 44 000 readers in over 172 countries.

Visit www.humancapitalreview.org

CONTENTS

ABOUT THE EDITOR

Johan Herholdt's most recent major project involved assisting a team with the development and delivery of a leadership development programme for a corporate and business bank. Since then he has decided to concentrate on writing and acting as facilitator rather than taking a more active role in the corporate world.

He is the author of a variety of business books and is a well-known Organisation Development and Change Enablement specialist in South Africa. He developed his views on knowledge assets as a knowledge worker in Human Resource Management in Mining, Insurance, the delivery of Televised Education and Training, Information Technology services, and Financial services.

His main areas of specialisation are systemic problem solving, change enablement programmes, personal growth and purpose development, as well as discourse processes and dialogics. Johan recently developed an "Energy Investment in Human Capital" programme with Johann Symington (to develop holistic wellness and prevent burnout), and has designed and delivered several large-group interactive events (the largest one being for 550 people).

With Knowledge Resources, Johan has published works on dialogue and facilitation (in the *Nuts & Bolts* series), as well as *Viable Business Strategies* in 2003 with Professor Marius Ungerer and Maurits Pretorius (the 3rd edition was published in 2011) and *Transforming Your Employment Brand* (with Laetitia van Dyk) in 2003. In 2004 he contributed a chapter ("Employment Brand – Four Bottom Lines and a Couple of Growth Engines") to *Building Human Capital – South African Perspectives* (edited by I Boninelli and TNA Meyer). In 2006 he co-authored *Leveraging Knowledge Assets* with Professor Marius Ungerer and Professor Koos Uys.

Apart from publishing articles, he speaks at conferences and teaches Archetypal Systems Thinking. He also mentors and coaches.

INTRODUCTION

When we prepare to go to work every morning, we rarely (if ever) think of the workplace as a unique learning environment with opportunities to continue life-long learning agendas. Today, more than ever, organisations realise the importance of providing development opportunities to people to motivate them, stay competitive and, ultimately, positively impact the bottom-line of business. Mentoring and coaching have come to be used more frequently in organisations to improve organisational competencies.

Having been mentored and coached during my career (often informally) and then coaching and mentoring others towards the end of my formal employment, I have often wondered if coaching, and (to a lesser extent) mentoring, was not just another fad. My own experience was that one could "feel" the difference in oneself, but did it really make a difference to the bottom-line? Could the effects be traced and a return on that investment be calculated?

Could the personal impact also have an organisational impact?

Marius Meyer tackles this question head-on in *The Bottom-line Impact of Mentoring and Coaching.* He explains why it is difficult, destroys some myths along the way, and cites the results of some international and national studies.

The next question that vexed me, especially as we started to design a company-wide programme for coaching and mentoring interventions, was whether there was any difference (other than cosmetic) between mentoring and coaching. **Kay Irissou** defines all the terms.

Of course, the next question is whether it really has to be one-on-one, or can mentors and coaches work with more than one person at a time, possibly even teams? **Andre van der Bijl** maintains that team-building techniques can be applied to increase the success of our mentoring and coaching efforts, and shows us how we can apply these principles.

1

Diversity is always something requiring thought and, like me, you may have wondered if mentoring and coaching could not be useful here. The *Human Capital Review* staff obliges by summarising the relevant chapters of *The Psychology of Coaching, Mentoring and Learning* by **Ho Law, Sara Ireland** and **Zulfi Hussain**.

To round off this introductory part, **David Clutterbuck** writes about coaching and mentoring, which have both come a long way in the past 40 years.

The next part of the book takes an in-depth look at **Mentoring**.

Niël Steinmann highlights some concerns about formal mentoring with which many of us grapple, and shows us how structured mentoring can work, despite the obstacles.

A mentoring relationship is often embarked upon by people from very different demographics and can be tremendously enriching for all parties, not to mention successful, too. **Cindy Dibete** and **Alex Misch** were paired by The Nation's Trust youth mentorship programme and give insights into mentoring from both perspectives – mentor and mentee.

Adel Du Plessis discusses the ways and means for the new generation of young executives to gain the maximum benefit from mentoring relationships, by reviving the apprenticeship ethos.

Mentoring can be a highly-effective, affordable developmental tool that delivers amazing results. **Penny Abbott** and **Peter Beck** highlight six flaws found in many mentoring programmes and show us how to correct them.

Marius Meyer shares snippets of the individual and collective wisdom of 30 HR mentors. Learning from the wisdom and experience of these mentors, we can identify new ways for growing HR practice in our organisations.

The next part of the book deals with **Coaching**.

Coaching has been around informally for many years. But as it is a new profession, you may be confused as to how to go about selecting a coach who is right for you and your particular needs. **Cindy Bell** gives advice.

Like death and taxes, constant change is one of life's few certainties. The rate of change this century has increased exponentially, and the ability to adapt to change is now a critical factor in the survival of organisations. So how do organisations use coaching to equip themselves to adapt to rapid change? **Samantha Stewart** answer this question.

Despite the current popularity of coaching, the value of coaches external to business has struggled for recognition. **Dale Williams** explains why, and also shows how to calculate the ROI.

In this insightful article, **Karel van der Molen** explores the concept of coaching, its many benefits in helping others to achieve peak performance, the qualities of a good coach, and the manager's role as coach.

Natalie Witthuhn Cunningham feels that action is needed to winnow out bad and ineffectual coaches. One way to assist in developing credibility for the profession is for the end users (the clients and organisations) to be rigorous in their selection process of coaches. Charlatans would then be weeded out.

Kathy Bennet and **Helen Minty** discuss the benefits of coaching and its role in building people's emotional intelligence and enhancing their personal and work-related life performance.

With clients on the lookout for approaches that will produce the best results with the smallest possible capital expenditure, it is a great time for those who use strengths-based coaching approaches. In this article, **Robert Biswas-Diener** introduces us to the strengths-based approach to coaching and educates us about some of the related background research. He goes on to explain some practical strategies for using this information in your own practice or organisation.

The next section in this book deals with the practice of using **Managers as Coaches**, adopting a so-called coaching style of leadership.

Antionette Gmeiner shares a case study to explain that coaching is the art of bringing out the greatness in people in a way that honours the integrity of the human spirit. It is both an innate human capacity and a teachable skill, which has now become a new way of working with people within a corporate context.

Many organisations are now expecting line managers to coach employees, but managers often find coaching difficult. The good news is that with the correct training and support, line managers can excel at coaching. **Penny Abbott** and **Peter Beck** show us how managers can be prepared to fill this important role. They provide us with a practical coaching model that can be readily applied within organisations.

Increased communication with more sharing and openness, the identification of personal areas for future development, skills improvement, and increased motivation. These are some of the spin-offs that one can expect organisationally when coaching managers to be coaches, not to mention the increased productivity which naturally results from good management–worker relations. **Helen Minty** and **Kathy Bennett** take us through their case study, which brings these and many other dynamics into clear focus.

We conclude with a short chapter about **Coaching Models**.

In a series of articles, **Dr Sunny Stout Rostron** introduces a variety of coaching models and gives examples of how to facilitate a coaching conversation using each one. In the first article, she focuses on the Purpose, Perspectives, Process Model and outlines how this model can be used to develop a structured approach to your coaching conversation, and how to contract with the client, structure the entire coaching journey and guide your coaching conversation.

In the second article she explores the nested-levels model of coaching, which first looks at the horizontal level of "doing", then goes a level deeper to "learning", and finally reaches a third "ontological" level, where new knowledge emerges about oneself and the world.

In the third article she examines the use of Otto Scharmer's U-process model for coaching individuals and groups.

How Can I Approach The Human Spirit? – The New Coach's Transformation, taken from *The Philosophy and Practice of Coaching: Insights and issues for a new era* by **David B Drake (Editor), Diane Brennan** and **Kim Gørtz**, is a profound lesson for coaches new and old.

We conclude with an example of a generic mentorship/coaching agreement by Kate Tucker.

The Editor

SECTION A

Mentoring and Coaching

- The Bottom-line Impact of Mentoring and Coaching: What is the ROI? by **Marius Meyer**

- Coaching and Mentoring – The Definitions by **Kay Irissou**

- Mentoring and Coaching Teams by **Andre Van Der Bijl**

- Coaching and Mentoring Diversity in Practice by **Ho Law, Sara Ireland and Zulfi Hussain**

- Next Decade of Coaching and Mentoring by **Professor David Clutterbuck**

The Bottom-line Impact of Mentoring and Coaching: What is the ROI?

by Marius Meyer

Calculating the return on investment in mentoring and coaching is measurably worthwhile and essential to success, explains Marius Meyer.

> **Marius Meyer** is the CEO of the South African Board for People Practices, the professional body for HR Management in South Africa (www.sabpp. co.za; contact Marius at marius@sabpp.co.za). He is also head of research for ASTD Global Network South Africa and an advisory board member for the Human Capital Institute (Africa). Marius is the author of 16 books and numerous articles.

Mentoring and coaching have grown significantly over the last five years, both internationally and in South Africa, to the extent that there have been hundreds of conferences and workshops on this important new leadership best practice. Now that we have started to implement some mentoring and coaching programmes in South Africa over the last few years, the question to address is: How can we evaluate the impact of mentoring and coaching?

For more than 15 years American companies have been inspired by the ASTD to measure the bottom-line impact of training and other human resource (HR) or capacity-building interventions. Return on investment (ROI) guru Jack Phillips defines ROI as a measure of the financial benefits obtained by an organisation over a specified period, in return for a given investment in a training programme. In other words, it is the extent to which the benefits (outputs) of training exceed the costs (inputs). If you have to spend (invest) R300 000 on coaching, what does the organisation get back for that investment? If the organisation does not get at least R300 000 back, you may have wasted the company's money with your mentoring and coaching initiatives.

Coaching impacts on not only the person being coached, but also the employees in the company receiving coaching from that individual. A research report by Whitworth and Shook (2003), from Case Western Reserve University's Weatherhead School of Management, shows that the impact of coaching-like training can last seven years. Manchester Inc recently released the results of a study that quantifies the business impact of external executive coaching. The study included 100 executives, mostly from Fortune 1 000 companies. Companies that provided coaching to their executives realised improvements in productivity, quality, organisational strength, customer service, and shareholder value. They received fewer customer complaints and were more likely to retain executives who had been coached. In addition, a company's investment in providing coaching to its executives realised an average ROI of almost six times the cost of the coaching.

Among the benefits to companies that provided coaching to executives, were improvements in the areas shown in Table 1 below.

Table 1: Benefits to Companies

Benefits to companies	Improvements
Productivity	53 per cent of executives reported
Quality	48 per cent
Organisational strength	48 per cent
Customer service	39 per cent
Reducing customer complaints	34 per cent
Retaining executives who received coaching	32 per cent
Cost reductions	23 per cent
Bottom-line profitability	22 per cent

Source: Whitworth & Shook (2003)

Among the benefits to executives who received coaching, were improvement in the areas shown in Table 2:

Table 2: Benefits to executives

Benefits to executives	Improvements
Working relationships with direct reports	77 per cent of executives reported
Working relationships with immediate supervisors	71 per cent
Teamwork	67 per cent
Working relationships with peers	63 per cent
Job satisfaction	61 per cent
Conflict reduction	52 per cent
Organisational commitment	44 per cent
Working relationships with clients	37 per cent

Source: Whitworth & Shook (2003)

Selected ROI results for mentoring or coaching, achieved internationally over the last couple of years and impacting on businesses, are shown in Table 3:

Table 3: Impact and study context

Impact and study context	Results achieved
Coaching at a hotel group (Phillips)	221 per cent ROI
Executive Coaching at Nortel Networks (Phillips)	788 per cent ROI
Executive Coaching (Metrix-Global)	500 per cent+ ROI
Mentoring and coaching (Conference Board)	600 per cent+ ROI
Coaching (Price)	529 per cent ROI
Survey of a hundred executives (Manchester USA Inc)	570 per cent ROI average
Training-travel saving due to coaching at Barclays (Pritchard)	£4 886 900

While some progressive companies have started to measure the ROI of their training programmes, the challenge now is to also measure the

ROI of mentoring and coaching interventions. Measuring the ROI of mentoring and coaching is a powerful way to show top management the value of these investments in financial terms. Using ROI methodology helps to answer the question: "For every rand invested in mentoring or coaching, how many rands does the employer get back?"

Many training departments have not yet made the extra effort to illustrate the payoff of their training programmes, let alone mentoring and coaching interventions. The good news is that the ROI can be determined through a scientific and professional approach to measurement. There are great rewards for such a measurement, as it gives the HR manager a powerful tool with which to report back to line management about the financial value of mentoring and coaching. This is in the language that line management likes – hard, tangible, quantifiable financial results – in rands and cents.

The interesting thing about ROI is that training managers know that ROI must be shown, yet very few actually do it. The following excuses for not calculating ROI have been provided by training managers during recent conferences organised by ASTD Global Network South Africa:

• HR and training managers do not know where to start.

• There is a lack of a measurement culture in training departments.

• They do not have the resources to calculate ROI.

• It is too difficult to measure the ROI of "soft" programmes such as leadership development, mentoring and coaching.

• It is too much effort to determine ROI.

• They are so preoccupied with all their training programmes and SETA requirements that there is no time to calculate ROI.

• They know that mentoring and coaching are good tools. Why measure what they know?

- They fear that if ROI is calculated, it will show that their coaching adds no value and that they will be at risk of losing their jobs! And what will happen to all the psychologists and management consultants who have overnight become "executive coaches?" Very few of them have been executives before.

Part of the above problem is that we are so preoccupied with focusing on assessment, due to the short-term imperative to meet the assessment requirements of SAQA, our SETAs and ETQAs, that we have forgotten about proper evaluation and measurement.

While assessment focuses primarily on the achievement of competence, measurement is needed to indicate the extent or lack of competence with specific reference to the organisation's tangible HRD benefits. In addition, the process of evaluation helps the HR development manager to decide how effective the overall training system is so that the necessary improvements can be implemented.

The following diagram puts the relationship between assessment, measurement and evaluation into perspective:

Evaluation

Assessment: Is the individual who has been coached competent? In other words, did that person meet the objectives of the mentoring or coaching agreement?

Measurement: Has the impact of the mentoring or coaching intervention been high or low? In other words, do you have figures that show an increase in outputs or performance? Are you able to convert these performance outputs into rand values? If you don't know, you cannot answer these questions.

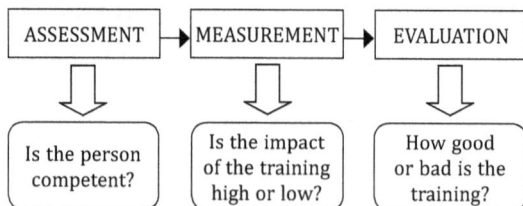

ASSESSMENT	MEASUREMENT	EVALUATION
Is the person competent?	Is the impact of the training high or low?	How good or bad is the training?

Evaluation: Now that the intervention is completed and you reflect back on the mentoring or coaching programme, how good or bad was it? What worked and what did not work? Are the coaches satisfied? Did the coach achieve his or her objectives? Is the manager of the coachee satisfied that the intervention made a difference?

Having been directly involved in a number of mentoring and coaching programmes over the past ten years, I ask myself the question: Why do so many of these well-intended programmes fail, despite the obvious business benefits of mentoring and coaching? I have spoken and interacted with more than one hundred training managers, mentors/coaches and mentees. The following reasons are often put forward:

- Management is often not committed to mentoring or coaching. They believe that they "came up the ranks the hard way. Why must the youngsters now get all the support and opportunities that they as managers themselves did not have?".

- Training managers know that their organisations need mentoring and coaching, but they do not know where to start.

- The rest of the organisation loses interest while they devote time to arguing and debating on the differences between mentoring and coaching.

- Mentoring and coaching are seen as the latest "buzzwords", and therefore are haphazardly adopted to align with what other companies are doing.

- There are too many providers in the market and many of them have totally different perspectives on how to implement mentoring/coaching. The market is thus confusing.

- Like other typical power plays, national attempts to "professionalise" the "coaching profession" has led to political infighting and turf battles between the leading consultants in the field. While some consulting firms have gained enormously from a financial perspective, the market has in the process lost out.

- Every second consultant these days has overnight become an "executive coach" or "life coach", and many of these people do not necessarily have the required credentials. In addition, the over-emphasis on "professionalisation", without recognising great mentors or coaches who have been doing excellent work for decades, defeats the object of skills transfer. Surely, it would be absurd to expect the Raymond Ackermans, Tokyo Sexwales and Cyril Ramaphosas of this world to "register" as coaches. They have already shown that they have what it takes to lead people and companies to great success.

- Learnerships have institutionalised "workplace mentors" as part of the learnership agreement, but in reality no or little workplace mentoring takes place. It is merely seen as a paper exercise signed off by the "workplace mentor".

- Mentoring and coaching is often viewed from a simplistic and one-sided perspective, while it is in fact a multidisciplinary field. It does not belong to psychology, industrial psychology, HR management, or any other specific subject discipline. Claims of exclusive ownership, and subsequent narrow one-sided implementation, have resulted in failure. Taking the best elements from psychology, business management, project management, leadership, HR development, general management, sport management, sociology, and other fields will produce a more integrated approach to mentoring and coaching. The time for protection and self-interest is over. Now we have to learn, share and empower – is that not what mentoring and coaching are all about?

- Mentoring and coaching "training" or capacity building is provided in the absence of a proper mentoring and coaching strategy and policy framework.

- No, or limited, skills transfer strategies are in place.

- Mentoring and coaching programmes are not aligned with the overall business strategy of the company. It is therefore not surprising that they are not seen as adding any value to the organisation.

- As a result of the above problems, we have forgotten about what matters most in mentoring and coaching – the development and growth of mentees and coachees!

Despite the reluctance on the part of training managers, there are a number of trends that have increased the interest and use of ROI for training, mentoring and coaching, and other capacity-building programmes in South African organisations:

- Owing to the promulgation of the Skills Development Act 97 of 1998, training budgets are growing. South African companies spent more than 3 percent of payroll on training, much higher than the international benchmark of 2,5 percent.

- Additional training and development programmes are being implemented as an aspect of companies' employment equity and workplace skills plans.

- Learnerships require a workplace component that learners complete under the guidance of workplace mentors.

- Several of the industry BEE charters have highlighted mentoring and coaching as initiatives to accelerate BEE in companies.

- Top management is exerting pressure on the HR function to show accountability in terms of tangible business benefits.

- The King II and King III *Reports on Corporate Governance* clearly highlights the importance of measuring the value of human capital development interventions. In addition, mentoring is mentioned as a critical intervention to support the sustainability of companies.

- Many companies are moving in the direction of outsourcing some or most of their training, with the result that training practitioners are beginning to realise that measuring the ROI of training can justify their existence in the organisation.

There are different options for measuring and evaluating mentoring and coaching interventions. For example, the perceptions of both mentors and mentees can be evaluated by means of questionnaires or focus group interviews. The knowledge of mentors and mentees can also be assessed by means of mentoring tests. In addition, it is also possible to conduct behaviour assessments to determine the ability of mentees to apply their knowledge and skills in the workplace. Ideally companies should use control and experimental groups to measure the impact of mentoring and coaching. However, few organisations have the time, resources and capacity to use elaborate research methods as part of evaluation.

The idea with ROI is to measure the impact of mentoring and coaching on organisational performance metrics such as higher productivity, fewer defects, better quality products/services, reduced costs, lower labour turnover, reduced absenteeism, and increased market share. All of these are tangible measures that can quite easily be converted to a rand value in order to determine ROI. Jack Phillips recently reported a 788 percent ROI on an executive coaching intervention at Nortel Networks. Several measures such as productivity, quality, cost control and product development time were used to calculate the ROI at the company. This figure is also consistent with the research by the Conference Board that has indicated a 1 : 6 ROI ratio for mentoring and coaching. In other words, for every dollar spent on coaching, companies get six dollars in return – not a bad investment at all!

There are several myths concerning mentoring and coaching measurement, particularly as far as ROI is concerned:

- **It is impossible to measure the ROI on mentoring and coaching, because we are focusing on soft skills.** Not true, we will show you that it can be done!

- **Every aspect of mentoring and coaching should be measured.** This is also not true – in many cases it is not necessary or desirable to measure mentoring and coaching. For instance, when a coachee walks out there with more self-confidence or a better attitude, you do not necessarily want to put a rand value to it. In fact, personal growth on that level is most likely immeasurable. No money in the world can equate to that.

- **You have to be a financial analyst or chartered accountant to measure the ROI of mentoring and coaching.** Definitely not true. The formula for ROI measurement is very basic.

- **If the ROI is low, it means that the intervention has failed.** Not necessarily, but it could indicate how the intervention can be improved upon. It may also indicate that your organisation's culture is not ready for mentoring or coaching.

- **ROI measurement on its own is enough to show the value of mentoring and coaching.** False – you need an integrated evaluation and measurement strategy for mentoring and coaching, as well as a skills-transfer strategy.

Contrary to popular belief, ROI measurement is not about numbers only. If you want a successful ROI measurement strategy in your organisation, you will realise that ROI is 90 percent about relationships and only 10 percent about numbers. In other words, if you have good relationships with your business managers, coaches and mentees, it should not be difficult to achieve the numbers. If the relationship is good, you can help them to improve on the numbers quite easily.

An integrated evaluation and measurement framework for mentoring and coaching is needed in South African organisations. The framework clearly indicates how mentoring and coaching interventions can be evaluated in the workplace. The integrated evaluation framework includes both soft and hard approaches to evaluation. It is based on the premise that you first need a sound mentoring and coaching strategy for the company, before you embark on capacity building. In addition, a clear skills-transfer strategy is needed to build skills-transfer activities into the framework – before, during and after mentoring and coaching.

The sustainability of mentoring and coaching in your organisation will depend to a great extent on the approach, process and results of evaluation and measurement.

I wish you success with your effort to convert powerful mentoring and coaching relationships into bottom-line ROI results for your company.

❖ ❖ ❖ ❖

Coaching and Mentoring – The Definitions

by Kay Irissou

In an ever-changing, fast-paced world, where dictionary definitions are slow to keep up or no longer apply, it is important to keep pace with the evolutionary meanings assigned to certain words and concepts, writes Kay Irissou.

> **Kay Irissou** is an independent life skills trainer; executive, business, relationship, teen and life coach; writer and speaker. She also facilitates life and business coach training and is involved in day-to-day HR and business-strategy work. She is a single mother, a lover of fine things, and has dedicated her life to pursuing wisdom from within. Her contact information can be found at www.kayirissou.co.za.

The word "coach" was originally used to describe a horse-drawn carriage; it was later used to describe one person helping another on a sporting field; and it has now evolved to include a person assisting another with life and business issues. Coaching can also be defined by its relationship with other approaches that appear to be similar, including:

- Managing

- Counselling

- Mentoring

- Teaching, and

- Training.

Many people use the term "coaching" interchangeably with these terms, creating some confusion about what coaching is and, more importantly, what it is not. The International Coach Federation describes coaching as, "An ongoing partnership that helps clients to produce fulfilling results in their personal and professional lives. Through the process of coaching, clients deepen their learning, improve their performance and enhance their quality of life".

Executive coaching

Executive coaching is aimed at inspiring executive leaders to make behavioural changes which transform themselves and the people around them, and thereby increase business results and performance.

"Executive Coaching is a facilitative, one-on-one, mutually-designed relationship between a professional coach and a key contributor who has a powerful position in an organisation. The coaching is contracted for the benefit of a client, who is accountable for highly complex decisions with wide scope of impact on the organisation and industry. The usual focus of the coaching is on organisational performance or development, but it may also contain a personal component." – Summary findings from the International Executive Coaching Summit, October 1999

Executive Coach Karol Wasylyshyn, in "Coaching The Superkeepers" (*The Talent Management Handbook*, 2003), confirms that "executive coaching is a company-sponsored perk for top high-potential employees. It is a customised and holistic development process that provides deep behavioural insights intended to accelerate an executive's business results and effectiveness as a leader. This coaching is based on a collaborative relationship between the executive, his or her boss, his or her human resources manager, and an executive coach".

Business coaching

A business coach works with owners of small to medium sized enterprises, focusing on the company's development and the client as an individual. Business coaching is the practice of providing support and occasional advice to an individual or group, in order to help them recognise ways in which they can improve the effectiveness of their business. It can be provided in a number of ways, including one-on-one tuition, group coaching sessions, and large-scale seminars. Business coaches are often called in when a business is perceived to be performing badly; however, many businesses recognise the benefits of business coaching even when the organisation is successful. Business coaches often specialise in different practice areas, such as executive coaching, corporate coaching, and leadership coaching.

Business coaching is not the same as mentoring, which involves a developmental relationship between a more experienced "mentor" and a less experienced partner, and typically involves a sharing of advice. A business coach can act as a mentor – given that he or she has adequate expertise and experience. However, mentoring is not a form of business coaching. A good business coach need not have specific business expertise or experience in the same field as the person receiving the coaching in order to provide a quality business coaching services.

Workplace coaching

Workplace coaching is designed to train managers in coaching their internal teams working either with direct reports, or with staff across an organisation. Managers often rely on training in order to improve staff performance, and while training and coaching both promote learning, they do so in different ways:

- Training is about teaching specific skills or knowledge, while coaching is about facilitating someone else's thinking and helping them learn by working on live work issues.

- Training usually takes place off-site or in dedicated training sessions, while coaching takes place in the office and, when carried out by a manager, can be integrated into day-to-day workplace conversations.

- Training is more typically carried out in groups, while coaching is usually a one-on-one process and is tailored to the individual's needs.

- Training is usually delivered by an external consultant or dedicated internal trainer, while coaching can be delivered by an external consultant or manager.

Although they are distinct activities, training and coaching can work very well when used together. One classic obstacle encountered in business training is the difficulty of transferring skills and enthusiasm from the training room to the workplace. Coaching is an excellent way of helping people apply what they learn from a course, to their day-to-day work.

What is life coaching?

Life coaching has roots in executive coaching, which itself drew on techniques developed in management consulting and leadership training. Life coaching also draws inspiration from disciplines that include sociology, psychology, positive adult development, career counselling, mentoring, and other types of counselling. The coach may apply mentoring, value assessment, behaviour modification, behaviour modelling, goal-setting, and other techniques when attempting to help their clients.

Life coaches are engaged by individuals. The coach will work with the client within the context of their whole life, and will look at a variety of areas depending on what the client wants to achieve. They may focus together on the client's creativity, health, career, finances or personal relationships. Life coaching is a practice that aims at helping clients determine and achieve personal goals. Life coaches use multiple methods that are aimed at helping clients to set and reach their goals. Coaching is not targeted at psychological illness, and coaches are not therapists or consultants.

Four standards and self-appointed accreditation bodies are internationally recognised: the International (ICC) , the International Coach Federation (ICF), the International Association of Coaching (IAC), and the European Coaching Institute (ECI). No independent supervisory board evaluates these programmes, and each is privately owned.

Clients are responsible for their own achievements and successes. A coach cannot and does not promise that a client will take any specific action or attain any specific goals. Many people believe that coaching is non-directive, and that the client always drives the progress and the direction taken. Many successful coaches, however, are highly directive, and a good coaching relationship is an ebb and flow of ideas and experiences.

Mentoring

Mentoring refers to a developmental relationship with a more experienced "expert" and a less experienced (and usually younger) protégé. The term "mentor" has been around for centuries, originally derived from a character in Homer's *Odyssey* who guides a young boy through a difficult time. Mentoring is instructional; it bestows new vocational skills and provides answers through the teachings of an expert. In the workplace, a mentor is usually a more senior person who shares experience and advises a junior person working in the same field. A mentor in the workplace is not typically the line manager of the person being mentored, but someone who is available for advice and guidance when needed.

Evolution

Whichever form of coaching or mentoring you choose for yourself or your business, it is important to know what it is that you would like to achieve and to make your decision based on that outcome. As a new and growing industry, coaching can be moulded to your specific needs and requirements. Rather than getting caught up in labels, choose an individual or company that is flexible to your needs.

❖ ❖ ❖ ❖

Mentoring and Coaching Teams

by Andre van der Bijl

Mentoring and coaching are not new human resource development tools. There is, however, a renewed interest in them and a concern about what makes mentoring and coaching work. Andre van der Bijl maintains that team-building techniques can be applied to increase the success of our mentoring and coaching efforts, and shows us how we can apply these principles.

Andre van der Bijl is Senior Lecturer and Programme Co-ordinator at the Faculty of Education and Social Sciences, Cape Town Peninsula University of Technology.

He has over eighteen years' experience in education and training, first as a lecturer at FET colleges and since 1994, in teacher education. He co-ordinates two programmes in the FET band, namely the Post Graduate Certificate in Education (PGCE: FET) and the National Professional Diploma in Education (NPDE: FET). Andre has a Masters and a Bachelors degree in Education from Stellenbosch University, as well as a Bachelor of Arts and Higher Diploma in Education (Commerce) Secondary from the University of Cape Town. He is currently busy with his PhD.

Andre can be contacted at bija@iafrica.com.

Sun Tzu, the ancient Chinese military philosopher, summarised the importance of teams and team building when he said that leading an army of 100 000 is the same as leading 10 people. The leaders of 100 000, he said, should each lead the representatives of 10 000, who each lead the leaders of 1 000, whose subordinates each lead 100, each of who leads 10.

A point noticeable when analysing principles applicable to mentoring and coaching, on the one hand, and team building and management on the other, is similarity. Both groups of processes require:

- The existence of a common goal

- Motivation

- Open communication channels

- Joint decision making

- Regular meetings

- Reward and review.

The current collective wisdom suggests that coaching and mentoring teams is not unlike developing and managing teams. However, the nature of the coaching and mentoring processes require a different focus to the conventional team building and team management process.

While conventional team building and management relies on the existence of a line of authority with a team working towards a common goal, coaching and mentoring is largely based on informal learning and periodic reflective interaction. This means that the group dynamics inherent in team building, in a conventional sense, are not present in a mentoring or coaching situation. The principles and processes involved in team building and management can, however, be successfully applied to coaching and mentoring.

Understanding team dynamics

The conventional perception of teams, expressed by management authors like JAF Stoner, is that the team is a fundamental unit of an organisation. Based on this perception, it is argued that the key to developing organisations is the building and development of sound teams.

Teams can be groups of people who work together on a permanent or indefinite based. Stoner called these *family groups*. Alternatively, a team can be formulated for the execution of a specific task. Stoner calls this type of team a *special group*.

Other publications provide different classifications of groups and teams and as a result, a number of frames of reference exist. The classification framework published by Stoner is applicable to mentoring and coaching as it focuses on the reason for the existence of groups.

The reason for the existence of the two types of teams differs and so too does the management of their activities, accomplishment of tasks, and management of relationships in the team and between the team and other teams. As the purpose of *family groups* is to exist over the long-term activities, team maintenance is the hub around which the team operates. In contrast, as *special groups* exist for the execution of a specific task, the task at hand its the hub around which the team exits.

Understanding coaching and mentoring

Coaching and mentoring are generally regarded as two of a set of on-the-job training mechanisms. Their appropriate use, however, has been the source of contestation amid allegations of questionable success.

Coaching can be described as a short-term-orientated process in which skills are developed through the interaction between a skilled person and another who is expected to master the skill. Mentoring is a broader process in which an identified master is tasked with developing mastery in others.

What characterises mentoring and coaching as human resource development tools and differentiates them from others, is that they involve informal learning. These two forms of learning have different origins, however. Coaching has its origins in the sports environment and traditional on-the-job training techniques. Mentoring, on the other hand, has its applicational origins in senior leader training and as a result, takes its name from the mythical character, Mentor, in Homer's book, *The Iliad*.

What differentiates the coaching and mentoring is scope. While mentoring has a broad, long-term professional development focus, coaching has a job specific, short-term focus. A practical differentiation between coaching

27

and mentoring is, however, difficult. As a result, many business training books on the subject use the two terms interchangeably, usually after providing descriptive differences. The term "coaching" is not used in some professional environments (such as education and nursing). Although the term "mentoring" is used in these environments, it is largely applied to on-the-job induction training.

As a result, partly because of the nature of mentoring and coaching as learning mechanisms and partly as a result of the grey area between the two, their success is open to question.

Implementing team-building and maintenance techniques

Case studies on mentoring and coaching programmes indicate that sometimes they work and sometimes they do not. A key factor in the success, or lack thereof, of mentoring and coaching programmes appears to be internal dynamics. Very often the implementation of coaching and mentoring programmes is left to voluntary co-operation between mentors and coaches and their subordinates. Mentors and coaches are often volunteers with time available. Alternatively, they may be people who have been identified as mentors or coaches. Where appointed mentors and coaches are not voluntary participants in the process, other elements of the work environment often receive precedence over meetings between mentors or coaches and their subordinates. The problem of meetings not happening is a topic that commonly features in mentoring case studies.

Implementing team-building and maintenance techniques, while not able to compensate for poorly constructed mentoring and coaching programmes, could be used to increase their success.

The key factors in applying team building and maintenance techniques are:

1. To understand the nature of the learning that is required. While there may appear to be a simple answer in the case of coaching, a simple answer is very often not forthcoming for mentoring.

2. To understand clearly the nature of the mentoring and coaching that is to occur during each phase of the team-building and management process.

An amount of knowledge on how people learn during the mentoring and coaching process does exist. Research suggests that learning which occurs during mentoring and coaching depends to a large extent on the reason for its existence. In some cases, the available research suggests that management's aim is to recycle power and to perpetuate an existing status quo in other cases, the aim is to realise protégés' own value systems or to assist them in the construction of meaning.

Commonly, the team building process is regarded as a four– to five-stage process. Terms commonly use to describe the phases are:

1. Identity formulation

2. Task or goal formulation

3. Bonding

4. Processing

5. Assimilation.

During the phases of identity formulation and task or goal formulation, the group and the reason for its existence are determined. During the phases of bonding, processing and assimilation, the group carries out the work required the determined objectives in order to reach.

The key to the success of the introductory phases, the team development phases, lies in defining the reason for the existence of the team, and the acceptance of its goals by the members. Acceptance of the goals requires acceptance of what is to be done as well as the way in which the goals are to be achieved.

Team maintenance mechanisms

The key to the achievement of the goals of the team, once work has started, is co-operation and ongoing development. Suggestions to encourage co-operation and ongoing development include the following three team-maintenance mechanisms:

- Regular meetings

- Reviewing processes with the aim of improving performance

- Joint decision making.

These mechanisms not only provide mentors and coaches with key subordinate development and motivation tools, but they also coincide with problems commonly listed as reasons for the failure of mentoring and coaching.

A number of case studies on disagreements between mentors and coaches and subordinates have been published. The nature of the disagreements ranges from simple disagreements about goals, objectives and strategies to disagreements about discourse and worldview. A similar feature is postponement and cancellation of meetings. While joint decision-making may not be achievable in the mentoring and coaching process, joint decision making as a goal remains advisable. Similarly, although regular meetings do not guarantee protégé development, a lack of meetings guarantees a lack of protégé development.

What is clear, however, is that team dynamics and cohesive loyalty develop a motivational force that results in action that would not occur if left to individuals.

The three-point team-building and maintenance process

The motivational force that develops out of team dynamics and cohesive loyalty can be used by mentors and coaches to increase the success of the processes they are expected to manage.

To illustrate how team dynamics can be used to promote mentoring and coaching, a three-point team-building and maintenance process will be used.

1. Team identity and goal or task formulation

This is the team-building process. During this phase, mentors and coaches have a few key tasks which will make or break the process.

The first key task is to determine the nature of learning that has to occur. Is the reason for the mentoring process to develop people who will continue the existing status quo, or is it to develop their own value systems? The answer to this question determines not only the nature, goals and tasks involved, but also which people should be mentored or coached and the power relations required. If the reason for the existence of a mentor or coaching process is to maintain an existing status quo, the pendulum of power and, as a result, decisions on process, structure and outcomes, lie with the mentor or coach. If, on the other hand, its reason is to develop the protégé's own value system, then the pendulum of power and resultant decisions lie with the protégé.

If the reason for a mentoring or coaching process is the construction of meaning, a shifting pendulum of power is required and, as a result, mobile milestones. Outcomes should, however, remain predetermined and clearly defined and contain detailed structural planning.

Case studies indicate that planning mentoring and coaching programmes, tends to be general, leaving the implementation of the process to informal interaction between individuals. Teaming up protégés with mentors or coaches not only saves on mentors and coaches; it makes it possible to exploit learning and synergy advantages that result from group learning. In other words, when mentoring or coaching is done with groups of people, they not only learn from the mentor or coach and through self- reflection; they also learn from each other, and learning is improved as a result. Group cohesion acts as an additional motivator to both the mentoring and the coaching process, as well as to learning. The end result, for both the process and for learning, is improved quality.

2. Bonding

Bonding, the second phase, involves the reaction of protégés to the team, its members, and the goals and tasks assigned. Protégés are not, or should not, be passive members of the coaching and mentoring process. As a result, they will develop a view of the mentor or coach, the reason for the relationship, and its outcomes and milestones. In the 1980s, educational sociologists used the term *"sussing out the teacher"* to refer to the development of teacher credibility in the minds of a learner. *Sussing out* the mentor or coach, as well as *sussing out* peers and the process, milestones and outcomes, is the expected response. A positive *sussing out* outcome is vital.

In a one-to-one mentoring or coaching process, positive *sussing out* of all aspects is vital. However, if groups are involved an in-general positive is sufficient. Partial negativity could be compensated by the group if the group as a whole is positive.

Group dynamics can be exploited not only in the development of group cohesion it can also be exploited in maintaining group cohesion, executing the mentoring or coaching process, and reaching its outcomes.

3. Processing and assimilation

Processing and assimilation, the third phase, involves carrying out the work required by the team. Bonding, processing and assimilation, as well as the phase of reflection that is included in some publications, are cyclically interrelated processes; they are not exclusive or linear.

Case studies indicate the results of the realities of interpersonal interaction in a dynamic business environment. Common shortcomings from case studies include the following scenarios:

- Mentors and protégés lose interest, especially if the process is carried out over an extended period of time or meetings are postponed or cancelled if other priorities develop.

- Milestones that were determined in advance or by external consultants prove to be irrelevant.

- Interpersonal conflicts develop.

- Mentoring or coaching is not listed as a performance management indicator.

Most of the shortcomings listed above can be eased through the use of team mentoring and coaching. Team dynamics contribute to the maintenance of interest in projects when individual interest ebbs and flows. It is also more difficult to postpone or cancel meetings established for groups than for individuals, as it is easier to justify team management as a performance than to justify one-on-one mentoring or coaching.

Conclusion

Mentoring and coaching are not new human resource development tools. There is, however, a renewed interest in them and a concern about what makes mentoring and coaching work. As mentoring and coaching have a strong qualitative component, it can be argued that qualitative management techniques could aid their implementation. One such technique is the utilisation of group dynamics and team management.

Teams develop dynamics, which may not only compensate for the inadequacies of one-on-one mentoring and coaching situations; they may also act as a mentoring and coaching multiplier. When coaching or mentoring occurs on a one-on-one basis, the focus of mentoring and coaching is the mentor or coach. If teams are mentored or coached, opportunities for peer mentoring and coaching develop. Furthermore, if reflective practice develops in a team, then self-coaching and self-mentoring could also occur. The multiplicative effect of team dynamics therefore doubles and potentially trebles mentoring and coaching possibilities.

❖ ❖ ❖ ❖

Coaching and Mentoring Diversity in Practice

by Ho Law, Sara Ireland and Zulfi Hussain

A summary of extracts from *The Psychology of Coaching, Mentoring and Learning* by Ho Law, Sara Ireland and Zulfi Hussain.

Ho Law, Chartered Occupational Psychologist, the Managing Director of Empsy Ltd and Research & Technical Director of Morph Group Ltd, is an international practitioner in psychology, coaching, mentoring and psychotherapy. He is a founder member of the British Psychological Society's Special Group in Coaching Psychology (SGCP), with strategic responsibility for the ethics of coaching psychology, and is also a consulting editor of *The Coaching Psychologist*. He is currently an honorary lecturer at Liverpool's John Moores University and an International Advisory Board member of the Coaching Psychology Unit, City University London. He has published over 40 papers and delivered over 100 workshops and conference seminars in the UK and abroad, including Barcelona, Brussels, Hong Kong, Paris, Stockholm, and Zurich. He has received numerous outstanding achievement awards including the Local Promoters for Cultural Diversity Project in 2003, the Positive Image (Business Category) in 2004, and Management Essentials Participating Company in 2005.

Sara Ireland is a Chartered Occupational Psychologist with a background in HR. She is the Innovation and Applications Director of Morph Group Ltd. She is a founder member of SGCP and has UK and international management consultancy and organisation development experience, as well as working as an Executive coach and programme co-ordinator.

Zulfi Hussain, Business and Marketing Director of Morph Group Ltd, is also Chief Executive, board member, and director of a range of businesses and charities in the UK and across the world. He is chair of the European Mentoring and Coaching Council (2006). Zulfi received the Director of the Year (2005) Award from the Institute of Directors.

We take you through the four stages of coaching and mentoring from a psychological point of view.

In a diverse environment, the definition of coaching/mentoring described in chapter 4 becomes more difficult as the term has become more diffuse in a large number of contexts. This is compounded by the many people using different media and where diverse meanings are applied (Nandram, 2003). So what does the mentoring/coaching research and practice describe in chapter 3 add to our understanding of learning in collaboration in applied contexts?

We know that goal-setting may help to structure the coaching/mentoring process, but it is not vital to its success. We know that self-efficacy is important in bringing about satisfactory outcomes in coaching/mentoring, but that the network of sub-components underpinning "can-do" attitudes may differ across cultures. In coaching/mentoring, the focus is on nurturing to help individuals reach their potential, and the locus of control is of partial use in establishing a sense of responsibility, but also in recognising the importance of interplay with others and our situation. The coaching/mentoring relationship is coachee/mentee-driven, so coaches/mentors have to take a back seat and facilitate the other person to explore themselves, others and their environment, and work out causality and consequence in that situation.

The nature of the quality of the relationship is emphasised in coaching/mentoring as a prerequisite for learning and satisfaction more than in other strands of development. Features that are regularly cited as contributing to that quality relationship are trust, commitment, authenticity, listening, time for critical reflection, positive regard and caring, boundary clarity and management, questioning and challenge. These go beyond the routine programmed and instrumental conditions for learning employed by other methods, and lie at the core of our coaching and mentoring process.

Perhaps the caveat to our model lies with some individuals who have felt marginalised in previous partnerships for learning and working.

In some diversity mentoring pairs, such as black and minority ethnic (BME) staff and individuals with disabilities, there is some preparatory work to be done, where individuals can accept themselves and trust their experience before they can trust someone else who does not share some of those elements. Such commonality may be a good basis to build rapport and develop more security and self-affirmation. As the research on interpersonal attraction has identified, this stage may be satisfactory in the short term only, and provide a springboard for new development and wider receptiveness to learning. When individuals want to move beyond empathy, they may require a greater focus on commonality of goals and values as a precondition for continued learning.

This stage of mentoring minority individuals lasts months rather than years; alternatively, they may take on multiple mentors as their confidence increases. This will not apply to all people, though. There is good sense in extending the choice of mentors from a range of diverse backgrounds and with a range of experience for that important minority in any mentee group. Time limits for the duration of relationships need to be flexible to accommodate different needs. In the same way that there may be preparatory stage in mentoring, there may also be some common mentoring journeys underpinned by core patterns. Once again, we see diversity in the mentoring journey – we may travel at different rates, perceive the experience slightly differently, get off one or two stops earlier – but there may be commonality about some of the landmarks along the way.

We propose that diversity mentoring can be expressed as a triangle, as shown in Figure 6.4.

The model comprises four stages, with stage 1 at the bottom working up to the top to number 4:

- Prerequisite stage for diversity mentoring

- Beyond homogenous empathy into mentoring

- Looking forward and making things happen

- Maturation as a diversity mentor champion.

Stage 1 – Prerequisite Stage for Diversity Mentoring

Validation of their story and experience with a person of high-grounded empathy and/or similarity/homogeneity in minority area prepares them to trust others as self-acceptance and belief grow.

What can you do to move them on to the next level? Train them as mentors and mentees to empower them with regard to the process, even if they have more skills to draw on. Help them to become aware of emotional intelligence and its impact in mentoring/coaching.

Some people move quickly out of this stage as they have already made the journey on their own, but others need much more time. Choosing a mentor with high similarity is very important.

Stage 2 – Beyond Homogenous Empathy into Mentoring

A new mentor or extended role for the mentor form stage 1. Often mentees will be ready to test their learning in different relationships. New relationships offer the opportunity for individuals to consolidate a sense of self, review experience from this perspective and find new ways to develop trust and honesty.

What can you do to move them on the next level? Give positive feedback about how they present themselves. Encourage them to take on enhanced roles in their work or try new things or situations. Encourage them to keep learning logs that describe the changes taking place – both internal and those observable to others.

Stage 3 – Looking Forward and Making Things Happen

Move beyond the past and an understanding of it to an exploration of new insights from individual experience, which can be leveraged to shape the present and future. Be ready to start mentoring others in their area of minority experience or junior staff from the general population, or other individuals who have travelled less far on the journey.

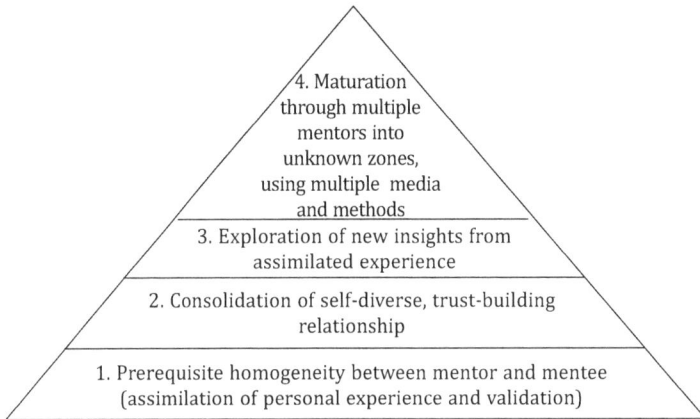

Figure 6.4 Diversity coach mentoring journey

What can you do to move them on to the next level? Supervision with other coaches, mentees and mentors, continual development and widening networks and roles/tasks is necessary. Particularly important is an increased tacit knowledge of how their environment works and, in an organisation how successful change is brought about, and the integration of how and why they have their minority experience and the skills and knowledge they can derive from it for the greater good. Use mentoring skills with a range of technologies and structures that go beyond established boundaries.

Stage 4 – Maturation as a Diversity Mentor Champion

- Mentor majority-culture people on diversity issues, showing real understanding of the environment and universal goals of engagement.

- Establish wide-ranging networks.

- Find new coaches/mentors to fit different purposes and manage boundaries well.

- Maintain roots in minority communities but also maintain diversity across communities.

- Cross-reference experience and bring creativity to whatever you do.

- Have a range of coaching mentoring relationships in place using different technologies.

- Use good practice and insights to inform wider universal practice and co-ordinate mentoring partnerships.

- Champion minority achievements.

- Offer input into new approaches and best practice.

- Be an observable role model across communities.

- Continue supervision and contribute to the development of others less far along the journey through training facilitation and strategic engagement at a wider level.

At this point, the focus is on maintenance rather than the next levels. People often drop out after a few years or, as a consequence of their success, become estranged from their minority community and find themselves in new roles where they cannot mentor as easily. Supervision and being mentored by someone with high homogeneity with you but less experience of the diversity/mentoring journey as one of your multiple mentoring relationships may help to avoid some of the pitfalls.

There have been a number of occasions when minority leaders who themselves have received mentoring may not be keen to offer it to others. In minority groups the effect shows up particularly in organisations, where minority leaders are in short supply. However, this is a universal finding across communities. It may be more about the insecurity of individual potential mentors, an over-alignment with the position and lead culture of players in similar positions they have attained, and the route that enabled them to get there. A co-ordinator of a mentoring programme reported that medical consultants were reluctant to mentor registrars in their development. She reported that they typically commented: "My colleagues and I got through on our own, and if they are any good, they will get through – it's how things are". A black consultant, when asked to mentor other BME mentee doctors, replied: "These schemes change nothing and that's why I don't get involved – although if you are really good you can get through to being a consultant."

While acknowledging specific differences among individuals, contexts and media, commonly-cited best practice from studies conducted in a wide range of mentoring and coaching situations referred to the importance of manual benefits, willingness to sign a mentoring agreement, preparatory training, and supervision. Clutterbuck (2003) summed up the best practice for mentors:

> *Matching needs to embody the element of choice, to offer at least two options to ensure commitment on either side. All relationships should be probationary for the first two meetings.*

Based on the psychological research presented in chapter 2 from a range of contexts, we cannot support the approach of trying to simulate aspects of face-to-face communication through video conferencing and technology as the way forward, as you lose some of the benefits of online communication. It may be that rather than trying to simulate face-to-face communication in a hybrid form, you should try to make the most of the medium of computer-based communication mix of methods (for example, phone, email, chat rooms, text, video conferencing, messenger) on the learning outcomes and individual learning style. What is the ideal ordering of any hybrid mix of communication in the process? What mix does not work? How is this affected by personal learning styles? What is the scope for more peer mentoring or team mentoring online, using group chat situations?

In this chapter, we put forward a model to explain the spectrum of the mentoring method mix. Furthermore, e-mentoring goes beyond distance mentoring. It is advantageous when cultural differences are wide and easily incorporated into organisation life and yes, there have been individuals who have owned up to e-mentoring several people at the same time. That may not be good traditional practice but as the mentor in question stated:

My mentees feel that I am attending to them entirely and I am, but the delay in the chat means that I can do two concurrently. Actually, I get ideas of questions and insights that I can use productively from one to another. Rather than distracting me, I find it stimulates my thinking and enables me to reflect back more effectively. I also know of mentees who like to run a mentee session concurrently with a session when they are mentored as they feel it enriches their experience in both roles.

It is also to be noted that in many e-mentoring schemes, a lot of the informal benefits are reduced by highly programmed and prescriptive schemes, which limit flexibility by allowing email only. Yet children are the chat-and-text generation, and it would be a shame if a medium in which they communicate fluently is not used because mentors feel less at home in that environment, or are less competent in designing systems that meet their needs. Many of the reasons given are concerns of protecting vulnerable mentees such as schoolchildren or vulnerable adults, and to fit in with pre-formatted, formal institution systems and protocols in communication and learning. Then there are design restraints, particularly costs, which limit the scope of specific e-mentoring programmes to optimise the range of styles and needs.

Although safety is always a concern, we must ensure that the merits of mentoring flexibility and fluidity are not lost. Technology should be optimised in a learner-centred way to inform mentoring options, and the preferences of mentees and learners should help us to overcome risks and barriers to their learning. All communication between children and vulnerable adults is risky, but the procedures on safety should not inhibit innovative design. If safety is considered at the outset, effective procedures can be developed that meet statutory and funding requirements. However, procedures need to be established which fit the purpose and the medium, rather than traditional mentoring procedures being tacked on to new approaches. We need to develop an integrated, safe culture for all vulnerable users, where children are informed how to keep safe boundaries and expectations are clear, monitoring focuses on breach of boundary codes, agreements are in place at the outset for randomised monitored e-mentoring, supervision for mentors and peer review for mentees are requirements, and mentees are trained as mentors to empower them with regard to the process so that they can assess their behaviour and outcomes.

As for coaching/mentoring neatly fitting into existing institutional arrangements, we have to remember that coaching/mentoring works best when it is informal and "outside the line". This may translate into schools and other institutions as being slightly apart from the mainstream but networked into the mainstream.

❖ ❖ ❖ ❖

Next Decade of Coaching and Mentoring

by Professor David Clutterbuck

Coaching and mentoring have both come a long way in the past 40 years. Although both have been around, in some form, as ad hoc, informal relationships for millennia, it is only during this period that they have become formalised, researched, structured and part of common vocabulary. So where have we got to?

Professor David Clutterbuck is one of Europe's most prolific and well-known management writers and thinkers. He is the author or co-author of more than 50 management books, one third of them on coaching and mentoring, and hundreds of articles on cutting edge management themes. Co-founder of The European Mentoring and Coaching Council, David also runs a thriving international consultancy, Clutterbuck Associates, which specialises in helping people in organisations develop the skills to help others. David is perhaps best-known in recent years for his work on mentoring, on which he consults around the world.

The broad scope of his work can be seen on the Clutterbuck Associates website at www.clutterbuckassociates.com.

David can also be contacted by e-mail on info@clutterbuckassociates.co.uk.

The state of coaching and mentoring today can be summarised in a handful of headings:

- *Definitional confusion*. The terms "coaching" and "mentoring" are sometimes used interchangeably. One organisation's definition of coaching can be another's definition of mentoring, and vice versa. The boundaries between coaching and therapy, in particular, are often vague. In large part, this is the result of different evolutions in coaching and mentoring in the United States (US) and Europe. Similarly, the term "life coach" can currently mean a highly-skilled coaching psychologist, or an aromatherapist who has attended a two-day workshop.

- *Different emphases of research.* Coaching has received much less research attention from academics. The bulk of coaching literature is qualitative. The few quantitative studies that exist are mainly focused on measuring the efficacy of executive coaching interventions, via self-report. Research validity and methodology are often poor. By contrast, mentoring research has been mainly quantitative. However, it also suffers from significant problems including failures of definition (being unclear about what is being measured), conflation of line manager and off-line roles, methodological issues (for example, over-reliance on self-report), and confusion between relationship descriptors or enablers, and relationship outcomes.

- *Multiplicity of professional bodies.* In the context of mentoring, there is no truly global representative body. In most countries, mentoring occurs on an ad hoc basis. The US has the International Mentoring Association which, like American football, has relatively little footfall elsewhere in the world. The United Kingdom (UK) has a Mentoring and Befriending Network, which is preoccupied with mentoring in schools and within the justice system. It has very little interaction with the European Mentoring & Coaching Council (EMCC), or the EMCC's UK branch, where the mentoring emphasis is primarily on business and employment applications. There are also regional mentoring networks in the UK which have useful websites, and integrate business and community mentoring[1]. The EMCC is the only international body to address coaching and mentoring equally as helping interventions. When it comes to representing professional coaches, however, there is a plethora of organisations, ranging from the highly reputable to the rather dubious. The main players internationally are the International Coach Federation (ICF), the EMCC (for Europe only) and the Association of Coaching (AC).

---

1   [Online] Available at http://www.mentfor.co.uk/ and http://www.scottishmentoring-network.co.uk.

However, there are also specialist groups representing particular interests – for example, the British Psychology Society has an active coaching subdivision aimed at promoting the role of psychology-qualified coaches.

- *Significant issues relating to quality.* The assessment centres that Clutterbuck Associates and others use to select pools of executive coaches for large employers confirm what many human resources directors already know instinctively – there are many more mediocre coaches in the marketplace than truly competent ones. Some are dangerous[2]. Although extensive work has been carried out in recent years to define coach competencies, this has not translated fully into coach training and accreditation. The attraction of the assessment centre is that it brings objectivity to a difficult process. By contrast, what people say in application forms or in interviews seems to be poorly indicative of competence. Measurement based on client satisfaction is also a poor indicator – self-reports of change are too easily conflated in executives' minds with simply enjoying having someone on board who will listen attentively, and empathise!

Increasing professionalism

The continued, positive collaboration and discussion between the main associations in this field looks set to deliver much greater clarity on what makes an effective coach. There are high hopes, for example, from the Global Convention on Coaching, an international network of experts in the field who are collaborating to develop a common body of knowledge.

There is, however, unlikely to be a single definition of either coaching or mentoring. Instead, we can see emerging a matrix of qualifications based on three areas:

- Level of skills requirement
- Nature of application
- Culture.

---

2   Berglas, S. 2002. The very real dangers of executive coaching. *Harvard Business Review*, 80(6):86–92.

The level of skills needed to be a professional executive coach, or a professional developmental mentor, for example, is different from that required in an "elder statesman" type of mentor. The latter may need little more than a lot of experience and a basic grounding in the use of non-directive helping styles. Equally, some types of coaching may require a level of behavioural change best serviced by a psychologically-qualified specialist. This, in turn, is a long way from the relatively basic level of skills required as coach by a line manager.

The application may vary substantially with context, where there are different ability levels of mentees to actively participate in managing the learning relationship. Compare, for example, a talent-pool mentoring programme for a large company, with a programme aimed at deprived teenagers.

Culture plays a role, too. The perspective that different cultures take on mentoring and coaching varies on a number of dimensions. Qualifications designed for a US marketplace will not suit Europe without considerable adaptation; nor is either likely to be an exact match for South Africa.

What this means in practical terms is that the versatility of coaching and mentoring is gradually being seen as a rich resource, rather than as an excuse for turf wars. Coaches and mentors in different situations require different qualifications, but these will gradually be mapped into broadly-agreed categories that will give clarity to practitioners, clients and HR purchasers alike. As a result, the name given to a particular style of coach or mentor will be less important than the aggregation or level of competency required.

The main threat to this scenario is a rearguard action by psychologists in the US, who have persuaded state legislatures to ring-fence any kind of helping intervention that may result in behaviour change. This pre-emptive land grab is being fiercely contested!

The accreditation of coach and/or mentor education leads inevitably to consideration of accreditation of supervisors. All the major bodies now expect professional coaches and mentors to be in supervision, although they are still edging towards a common definition of what this means. The EMCC, AC and ICF have a combined European working party that aims to establish common standards for supervisor training.

In mentoring, we will in the future see standards to regulate the qualifications and training offered to programme co-ordinators – a vital resource in making programmes deliverable. We already have international standards against which to benchmark mentoring programmes[3].

Increasing incidence of non-traditional forms

The standard US hierarchical model of mentoring still exists, but the trend around the world is for less directive, more egalitarian relationships[4]. E-mentoring and e-coaching have been found to reduce the impact of power differentials between participants. Initially dismissed by many coaches and mentors as a pale imitation of face-to-face learning relationships, e-mentoring and e-coaching have in fact proved highly effective. They offer a different, asynchronous alternative, in which time to think between questions and answers is built into the process. By contrast, we find that telephone coaching and mentoring have few of the advantages, and many of the disadvantages, of face-to-face and virtual relationships. While very effective practitioners can make a telephone session work, this is unfortunately not the norm.

Another innovation of recent years is upward mentoring, in which the hierarchically more junior person is the mentor and the senior person the mentee. Sometimes called "mutual mentoring" to further reduce any sense of power differential, organisations use this in particular to educate leaders about issues such as diversity.

---

3   International Standards for Mentoring Programmes in Employment, available at http://www.ismpe.com.

4   Hamilton, BA. and Scandura, TA. 2003. "Implications for Organizational Learning and Development in a Wired World". *Organizational Dynamics* 31(4):388–402; Harrington, A. 1999. *E-mentoring: The Advantages and Disadvantages of Using E-mail to Support Distant Mentoring*, available at www.coachingnetwork.org.uk/ResourceCentre/Articles/viewarticle,asp?artId=63.

Team coaching will also become a more mainstream corporate activity. By team coaching I mean the collective development of the team together, rather than individual coaching of each member. When Clutterbuck Associates researched this area recently[5], we were surprised to find almost no empirical studies. We found a lot of confusion between team coaching and team facilitation although the nature of the learning dialogue, and the purpose and duration of the intervention, are very different. We also found a number of organisations offering training in team coaching, but an absence of an evidence-based body of knowledge to support any learning assumptions.

As more research is carried out and as universities begin to deliver team-coach training for the working environment, we can expect to see greater clarity around the competencies required; these appear considerably broader than for individual coaching, and senior managers will need to acquire team-coach skills as part of their own career development.

Coaching and mentoring culture

Recently published research[6] has found that the primary difference between high-performing leadership teams and their so-so counterparts is the amount of time and energy they invest in coaching, mentoring and other forms of mutual development. Over the past five years, we have learned a lot about how to establish and sustain a coaching and/or mentoring culture. All the usual suspect characteristics are necessary – consistent support and championing from top management, and having a clear business case for why investing time and effort in coaching and/ or mentoring is important – but there are other factors, too.

One is to recognise that all managers and their teams are part of a system. Sending the manager on a sheep-dip training programme is almost certain to fail, because both the manager and his or her direct reports (and sometimes other stakeholders, such as the manager's boss)

---

5   Clutterbuck, D. 2007. *Coaching the Team at work.* London: Nicholas Brealey.
6   Wageman, Ruth, Nunes, DA., Burruss, JA. & Hackman, J. 2007. *Senior Leadership Teams: What it takes to make them great.* Harvard Business School Press.

need to change expectations and behaviour as well. It's always easier to snap back into habitual behaviour, unless the entire system (that is, the team as a whole) is helped to change at the same time.

We've also learned that training coachees is as important as training coaches, because coaching is an activity you do with someone – not to them. Giving coachees the right to demand coaching, when they need it, creates a very different dynamic from what we usually find in organisations.

In future, therefore, we expect to see a lot more attention given to changing organisational systems, making training an on-demand "drop down", and providing easily accessible resources to enhance knowledge and skills. Part of this will come from better online resources, and part from having coaching and mentoring role models throughout an organisation, whom to managers can turn when they need support or advice in their own developmental conversations with direct reports.

An important part of the change of culture will also be the rehabilitation of thinking time or reflective space during the working day. It's still common in most organisations for anyone who is quietly thinking to be given something else to do on the assumption that he or she is not doing anything useful. Yet effective "knowledge workers" need at least three blocks of 20 minutes or so each working day to lend focus to their work.

Cold turkey for goal junkies

One of the revelations in the past two years for my co-author, David Megginson, and I, has been that much of what we have been taught about the role and importance of goals at the beginning of coaching and mentoring assignments is simply not true! Hundreds of books have been written based on GROW (Goal, Reality, Options, Will), yet only a handful have dared to question whether there was evidence behind the assumptions that the one-to-one learning process has to start with a goal.

Now there is evidence. And it tells us that – except in very specific circumstances of short-term performance goals tied to a well-defined task – GROW is a dangerous distraction. The reality is that, in a healthy developmental relationship, goals emerge gradually. Expecting the mentee or coachee to begin with a goal obliges them to come up with something that will satisfy the coach and their boss. How committed they are to this goal is another matter!

In a recent study of mentoring relationships over time[7], Clutterbuck Associates measured goal clarity, goal commitment, and goal alignment (a broad sense of purpose, linked to both individual and organisational objectives) at the beginning of the relationships, and compared these to the relationship experience and outcomes for participants. While goal alignment did correlate reasonably well with both relationship quality and mentee outcomes, this was not the case for goal clarity or goal commitment, which showed no significant correlation with either.

Additional evidence continues to accumulate that too narrow a focus on specific goals "dumbs down" the relationship and results in participants not noticing other opportunities, which may help the learner achieve broader, more important goals[8]. The majority of experienced coaches, exposed to this research, profess relief at being "released from the tyranny of goals". I expect this critical re-evaluation of the role of goals to continue to gather pace, and lead in turn to more holistic perspectives on associated development practices, such as performance management.

Future research agendas

The arrival on the scene of a number of international journals in coaching and mentoring is one of the factors helping to speed up the exchange of ideas and good practice, both in the management of coaching and mentoring and in the crafting of more robust, more relevant, more credible research. A great deal of time and energy was wasted in the 1990s and

---

7   Clutterbuck, D. 2007. "A longitudinal study of the effectiveness of developmental mentoring". Unpublished doctoral thesis, King's College London.
8   Megginson, D. 2007. "An own-goal for coaches". Paper to UK Annual Conference of the European Mentoring and Coaching Council, Ashridge; Spence, G & Grant, A. 2007. "Professional and peer life coaching and the enhancement of goal striving and well-being: An exploratory study". *The Journal of Positive Psychology,* 2(3):85–194, July.

early 2000s in arguments between academics and practitioners over the relative value of formal (structured) mentoring versus informal (unstructured) mentoring. In the past few years, this has been resolved with the recognition that the level of formality or informality is merely a side issue – what counts is the quality of the relationship, whatever the context.

There is now so much research in mentoring (albeit of highly variable value) that this kind of pragmatic re-appraisal is perhaps inevitable. Moreover, researchers in coaching seem to be learning from the mistakes of their mentoring counterparts. We expect to see a lot more research grounded in the practical experience of coaches, mentors and organisations; and many more studies that utilise both qualitative and quantitative methodologies.

Some of the themes that remain to be explored include:

- What actually happens within the confines of the coaching or mentoring meeting? How do mentors and mentees perceive the social exchange at key points in the relationship? What are the implications of convergent and divergent perceptions?

- What are the critical success factors underlying mentoring and coaching programmes?

- What is the mechanism by which goals are established within developmental relationships, if not at the beginning? Can the relationship flourish independent of goals?

- What is the value of role modelling?

- How do mentoring and coaching support each other?

- Do coaching relationships have similar phases to those in mentoring?

- How can line managers acquire the objectivity to coach effectively, when the main problem in a direct report's performance may be the line manager him- or herself?

- How does supervision in coaching and mentoring differ from supervision in other disciplines, such as counselling?

And there are many more themes. The dominant impression of research in this field, so far, is often one of sterile repetition of similar studies with minor variations, using instruments often of dubious reliability or relevance. That is changing. There are new instruments, new perspectives, new questions. We can expect a considerable amount of our assumed wisdom to be challenged over the next decade, which will enrich both the practice of individual coaches and mentors and the design and implementation of coaching and mentoring in the workplace.

References

1   [Online] Available at http://www.mentfor.co.uk/ and http://www.scottishmentoring-network.co.uk.

2   Berglas, S. 2002. The very real dangers of executive coaching. *Harvard Business Review*, 80(6):86–92.

3   International Standards for Mentoring Programmes in Employment, available at http://www.ismpe.com.

4   Hamilton, BA. and Scandura, TA. 2003. "Implications for Organizational Learning and Development in a Wired World". *Organizational Dynamics* 31(4):388–402; Harrington, A. 1999. *E-mentoring: The Advantages and Disadvantages of Using E-mail to Support Distant Mentoring*, available at www.coachingnetwork.org.uk/ResourceCentre/Articles/viewarticle,asp?artId=63.

5   Clutterbuck, D. 2007. *Coaching the Team at work*. London: Nicholas Brealey.

6   Wageman, Ruth, Nunes, DA., Burruss, JA. & Hackman, J. 2007. *Senior Leadership Teams: What it takes to make them great*. Harvard Business School Press.

7   Clutterbuck, D. 2007. "A longitudinal study of the effectiveness of developmental mentoring". Unpublished doctoral thesis, King's College London.

8   Megginson, D. 2007. "An own-goal for coaches". Paper to UK Annual Conference of the European Mentoring and Coaching Council, Ashridge; Spence, G & Grant, A. 2007. "Professional and peer life coaching and the enhancement of goal striving and well-being: An exploratory study". *"The Journal of Positive Psychology,* 2(3):85–194, July.

❖ ❖ ❖ ❖

SECTION B

Mentoring

- Does Formal Mentoring Really Work? by **Niël Steinmann**

- Insights into Mentoring by **Cindy Dibete** and **Alex Misch**

- Mentoring to Retain Talent by **Adel Du Plessis**

- Why are Mentoring Programmes in South Africa Not Delivering? by **Penny Abbott** and **Peter Beck**

- Wisdom from Professional HR Mentors: Transferring Knowledge from One Generation to the Next by **Marius Meyer**

Does Formal Mentoring Really Work?

by Niël Steinmann

Mentoring has become a strategic business initiative and organisations are more than ever expecting to see a "return on relationship". Niël Steinmann highlights some concerns about formal mentoring that many of us grapple with, and shows us how structured mentoring can work, despite the obstacles.

Niël Steinmann is a specialist business consultant with extensive experience in the human resources field. He is a registered Industrial Psychologist and the founding member and director of People's Dynamic Development, a management consultancy that utilises African analogies to develop people and organisations so that they can significantly increase their performance capacity.

As a keen conservationist, he started his studies on animal behaviour in 1996, with a special interest in lions. Since 1998, Niël's close involvement and interaction with more than 30 different lions has provided him with valuable insight and knowledge on animal behaviour. This unique combination of knowledge, skills and experience has affirmed Niël as a recognised consultant in Southern Africa with an impressive client record. His clients include a list of notable South African and international companies. He is also a regular speaker at local and international conferences.

For more information, visit his website: www.peoplesdynamic.co.za.

As mentoring gains popularity, organisations need to consider carefully this powerful tool for developing employees.

Sometimes traditional models of mentoring have failed to keep up with trends in business. Mentoring has, however, become a strategic business initiative; and organisations are more than ever expecting to see a "return on relationship". It is for this reason that organisations have "institutionalised" and formalised mentoring. Relationships are expected to extract greater value-add for their growth and development!

However, we should recognise that "institutionalised mentoring" really grew from observing the unquestionable benefits that resulted from mentoring relationships – the result of a natural affinity between two people.

Structured mentoring

Questions keep on emerging from this "structured/formal" mentoring landscape, as initiatives and so-called mentoring relationships often fall short of not only organisational expectations, but even those of the mentor and mentee. Some of these questions are:

- Should mentoring be thought of as a central strategy involving people development, rather than a mere tool for a selected few in the business?

- Must mentoring be part of good management practices, and is it a role that managers should be expected to fill?

- What does it take to be a successful mentor, and how should a faculty of competent mentors be identified?

- How do we prepare mentors for this challenge?

- How do we encourage ordinary business relationships to show potential to turn into profitable mentoring relationships?

- How do we measure the success of such an initiative?

So what are the challenges of a structured/formal approach? Seven key questions highlight the concerns that organisations and those that implement formal mentoring grapple with.

1. Why are we doing this?

This becomes the most important question to answer before any attempt at institutionalising mentoring. For some organisations, mentoring is about ensuring competitiveness, sustainability and growth by fast-tracking high-potential employees for definite positions. Others employ mentoring as a vehicle to develop and retain a leadership pipeline for critical positions within their business. Some proactively invest in graduate development not only to ensure a more demographic reflection of society, but to develop a bench of talented young individuals as their business expands and grows.

A concerning trend is that organisations are willing to chase numbers in mentoring at the expense of profitable relationships. Most organisations pursue the value of mentoring without, in my view, clearly defining what it is that they would like to achieve. This not only makes it difficult to measure the true impact, but relationships (mentors/mentees) are expected to "make it work" without the necessary structure or end in mind!

2. Who should the mentors be?

Finding the right mentors is possibly the greatest challenge for organisations that are pursuing a structured mentoring programme. Implementers of mentoring programmes will testify that they have tried just about everything to engage the heart and minds of subject matter experts, line managers, and operational staff to fill a mentoring role. Imagine an organisation where nothing happens without support from the top, where a "project code" is necessary to engage employees' energy and time, where employees' timesheets and KPAs become the means by which they are rewarded – and people development is not one of those! The most successful mentoring relationships develop seamlessly without any form of "coercion", manipulation or incentive!

Jack Welch said: "You can't force managers to love and care for people. It must come from the heart! Mentors have a different gene." He describes this gene as "a love to see people grow, they get a kick out of seeing people being promoted, they celebrate their people, and have a generosity of spirit, they are not afraid to have strong people around them, and have an abundance mentality when it comes to sharing knowledge, experience and lessons from life".

Insightful mentors understand that, when they invest in their protégés, they help to shape the future and contribute to the sustainability of their organisation. The reality is that without a pool of competent and willing mentors, any mentoring initiative is doomed to fail.

3. How should we match mentors and mentees?

Many seasoned mentors believe that a structured approach is "artificial" and based on a formal agreement. The two parties do not come together as a result of a relationship that has grown organically into that of mentor–mentee. Such a structured relationship is often a result of a relationship thrown together arbitrarily, even when there has been an attempt at match-making.

Talking about the match, a mentor should have a natural affinity for the mentee. This is critical to the success of the relationship. This can unfortunately not be accurately predicted, nor authentically manufactured in a matching process. More often than not, both mentors and mentees find their meetings awkward and even stressful as a result of this "forced" intimacy. Predictably, involvement tends to peter out, and the so-called mentoring relationship is degraded to nothing more than a "now-and-then coffee session".

4. Does the success of formal mentoring depend on the mentee?

Mentoring should also be embraced as a vehicle for personal development by those benefiting from it. Mentees should exhibit particular qualities and demonstrate "character" in order to maximise a relationship that could potentially make a significant impact in and on their lives and careers. Yet for mentoring to be "profitable", the relationship needs to be characterised by common ground, high levels of trust and openness that is reciprocal over time.

A "profitable" mentoring relationship differentiates itself from other working relationships in its level of intimacy, since it deals with a number of crucial conversations and fairly sensitive topics, such as managing relationships, social graces, negotiating the company's political landscape, and personal growth and feedback. The above is in my view the responsibility of both the mentor and mentee.

The question remains: does a formal mentoring programme/relationship create expectations that dampen the eagerness and hunger of the mentee? All those "natural" relationships have evolved because of both parties seeing something in the other, and then seamlessly pursuing the value of that which lies at the heart of the relationship, be it professional supervision, career advice, networking opportunities, or greater business exposure.

5. How much structure is necessary?

To preserve a formal mentoring relationship, it may be necessary to provide templates, guidelines, and review meeting support. My corporate endeavours highlighted the challenge of this dichotomy. The structure that is provided to assist relationship A becomes the reason that it dampens the spontaneity in relationship B. This will differ not only from relationship to relationship but also from organisation to organisation. The outcomes of the programme must dictate, and the unique culture of the business should guide, how much structure would be sufficient without overloading the relationship.

6. How do you sustain formal mentoring relationships?

The reality is that formal mentoring relationships need support to help to protract the relationship, but more so to ensure that the benefits of the mentoring relationship are met. This is the true challenge, because some organisations are willing to invest in such an initiative only if there is a "return on relationship". This in itself is a challenge, but more so when the culture in the organisation contradicts the value of people development. It is when operational efficiencies, business excellence, profit margins and bottom line results take priority to or over everything else that mentoring relationships suffer most!

7. How do we measure the success of mentoring?

It is simple; the value of a structured mentoring programme lies in the fact that it is more measurable than those that evolve naturally over time. This is the reason that organisations are willing to invest in such an initiative. Some relationships have a strong "time-to-competence" outcome, where mentees are assessed against specific performance results in their field of expertise. Others are linked to accelerated learning, where leadership assessments, employee satisfaction surveys, and even operational performance of the business are key measures. There are countless other measures, such as staff retention, promotions, complexity of projects and assignments, and readiness on succession planning grids. All of these measures should be derived from the initial question: why are we doing this?

Organisations need to have the maturity to measure the true impact of mentoring long after the formal relationship has "expired". It is only then that the tangible benefits of "profitable relationships" have matured. Yes, the veritable value of mentoring lies beyond the time frame of a specific mentoring relationship, and it is evident in successful mentees' performance, their level of accountability, and their leadership influence. The "return on relationship" lies in the projects that they manage, the business they generate, the revenue stream they secure, and even the complexity of a project they manage. Can all of this be attributed only to mentoring? Probably not, but most of these mentees will bear witness to the mentors in their lives and the contribution and mark that these extraordinary people have left!

Thoughts to consider

Clearly, structured mentoring relationships are exposed to a number of individual, interpersonal and organisational challenges. These factors loom large in any mentoring relationship, and it is for this reason that I believe that it is important to highlight these realities during mentor and mentee training. It is furthermore critical to build the capacity of both mentors and mentees to maximise and leverage learning within a structured mentoring environment.

Despite these challenges, I have witnessed scores of structured mentoring relationships that have presented phenomenal growth results. Mentees will testify that they have been products of such mentoring relationships, and here is the true value: the best way to reward a mentor is to become one for others. It is when formal relationships work that they contribute to a culture where people informally pursue the value of mentoring as a development tool. Mentors publicly proclaim the importance of mentoring and the benefits they themselves gained from such relationships. They encourage others to experience the pleasure in seeing mentees develop, grow, and ultimately succeed (whether formally or informally, short or long term, or whether as a result of a single action or an agreed-upon development plan).

The success of a structured mentoring relationship (like any other) depends on both parties' commitment to meeting the challenges of the relationship and to taking full advantage of the opportunities that are presented – all of this with a clear end in mind for the relationship!

Remember, mentors never stop mentoring – that is the difference between success and significance. In John Maxwell's words: "Significance is when I add value to others … I think mentoring is significance…"

Inasmuch as mentors leave something behind, they help to shape a better future for us all! Mentoring relationships, in a much broader context, create sustainability for the future of families, communities, and our country.

❖ ❖ ❖ ❖

Insights into Mentoring

by Cindy Dibete and Alex Misch

A mentoring relationship is often embarked upon by people from very different demographics and can be tremendously enriching for all parties, not to mention successful, too. Cindy Dibete and Alex Misch were paired by The Nation's Trust youth mentorship programme, which specialises in pro bono placements and supervises these relationships throughout. For two years they worked together, and both gained invaluable insights and achieved marked success.

> **Cindy Dibete**, principal of D'bete Financials, is a member of the South African Institute of Professional Accountants. Contact Cindy on cindy@dibete.co.za.
>
> **Alex Misch** is a qualified lawyer and is currently employed as the legal manager of the South African subsidiary of a global IT outsourcing company. He has also been involved in a number of coaching and mentoring projects as well as several entrepreneurial ventures. He is as passionate about South Africa as he is saddened by what he considers to be the heart-rending waste of human potential, energy and passion of the people of this incredible country.

By the middle of 2005, D'bete Financials, a small accounting firm situated in the heart of Braamfontein, Johannesburg, was in a precarious financial state. What had started out as a dream for its owner, Cindy Dibete, was fast turning into a nightmare. A failed attempt to open a branch office (in the hope of generating additional revenue) had drained the young business of much-needed cash and management attention. Staff turnover was high, morale was low, and cashflow was at a critically low level, added to which, the office IT infrastructure was unstable and the telephone system unreliable. Clients consisted mostly of sole proprietors of start-up and micro-enterprises with poor management and even worse payment records, and for whom accounting services were grudge purchases, the need for which was imposed on them by law.

63

In need of finance and advice, and almost ready to give up, Cindy approached The Nation's Trust youth mentorship programme for assistance. She obtained a small loan and was paired off with a volunteer mentor, Alex Misch, an attorney and Gordon Institute for Business Sciences (GIBS) graduate who had volunteered for the programme.

Over the following two and a half years, Cindy and Alex worked together as a dedicated team, meeting almost weekly during the first year, and bi-weekly thereafter. Today D'bete Financials is a thriving practice that has dramatically increased its turnover, cut its costs, runs on proper systems, controls and processes, and has a vastly more profitable client base.

In March 2008, Cindy and Alex presented their story to the Knowledge Resources Mentorship Conference. They were asked to name the critical success factors that had made this particular relationship so successful. Listed below, find some of the highlights of their story.

- **Mutual expectations**

Of the first meeting with Cindy, Alex says:

*"When I met Cindy, I was terrified. It was my first assignment as a volunteer mentor and, quite frankly, I felt the weight of the world resting on my shoulders. I had no idea to what extent Cindy would make me responsible for the success or failure of her firm, or how uncritically she would rely on what I was able to offer her; or even how **entitled** she would be to rely on what I gave her. The potential failure of this relationship appeared huge. There were questions of race, culture and gender; not to mention the fact that we came from different professions and that we were both busy people. There was no doubt that we would need to make a very deliberate effort to make this relationship work, and the question was whether we would **both** be willing to put in the time and energy to make it happen. In other words, I had no idea what to expect; and even less of an idea of what Cindy would expect from me."*

Cindy says:

"I also had no idea of what to expect, and even less of an idea of what mentoring actually was. All I knew was that I needed someone to tell me what I was doing wrong and I hoped that Alex would be able to assist me with that."

It was fortunate that both their expectations ultimately complemented each other very well. Alex says that in Cindy he found someone with an incredible sense of curiosity and a thirst for knowledge. *"Cindy is one of those people who is able to take what you give them, analyse it, apply what is useful, and discard the rest – and then take responsibility for the outcomes."*

According to Cindy, *"Alex was able to offer me incredible insight into the profitability drivers of my business. In fact, to this day I still use the models he gave me to make many of my business decisions. But he did not expect me to take as gospel what he gave me. He gave me the room to make my own decisions – without any judgement, interfering ego, or personal agenda."*

- **Commitment to the relationship**

According to Cindy and Alex, there were various elements to their commitment to the relationship. For one thing, they were both prepared to set aside a regular time slot on Friday afternoons, which became almost inviolable. *"I think that during the first six months we may have missed one or two sessions,"* recalls Alex, *"but essentially this was one of those items in **both** of our diaries that generally, quite simply, could not be moved."* Not only that, Cindy remembers that on more than one occasion she asked Alex for assistance outside of those regular time slots, which he willing gave – for aspects such as recruitment interviews, exit interviews, marketing advice, tender reviews, and strategy sessions.

Another dimension to their mutual commitment was the willingness, by both of them, to take responsibility for the relationship as well as for the inevitable setbacks and successes.

Alex comments:

"One of the ingredients of this relationship was Cindy's willingness to ask for help. Many people are afraid to ask for "even more", even though they know that what they should ask for is of critical importance at the time. For my part, I must say that I was incredibly lucky in that D'bete Financials always had great potential. I have worked in companies with millions of rands at their disposal, but whose failure was pre-programmed into their business model and management team. I wanted Cindy to succeed. I felt that her success would reflect on my ability as a mentor. So, if something went wrong, we would both be responsible. And I truly admire Cindy for her willingness to take responsibility."

- **Goal setting**

Cindy believes that this is probably where the hard skills of their little team came into play. It was a question of both of them being able to identify and agree on the problem, determine its priority, decide on a plan of action, and combine all this with targets and schedules. *"Not many people like to be told what's wrong with their businesses – and then, further, to be supervised in fixing those problems,"* says Alex, *"and I believe that you can do that only if you have true consensus on the problem, its priority, and how to fix it."*

- **Personal rapport**

Cindy and Alex both say that they like each other as people, though it is less clear to them what role a personal affinity may have in the success or failure of a mentoring project. *"It may certainly make things easier, particularly when it comes to commitment and taking responsibility,"* says Cindy, *"but what is even more important, I think, is mutual respect, and possibly even a form of admiration of sorts."* Of that there seems to have been no shortage.

"I have always admired people with spunk and courage – and particularly entrepreneurs," comments Alex. *"Here you have a black female accountant, who could have walked into just about any one of the big*

accounting firms and written her own cheque, and she chose to follow her dream, with that rare mixture of humility and ambition. Her pride and sense of ownership in her business, coupled with her willingness not only to take advice but to implement it, just blew me away. And she has a family to take care of! She could have taken the easy route, but decided to stay true to herself. I admire that."

For her part, Cindy says, *"Alex took me back to school, to all those MBA classes that I seem to have missed, and he gave me an analysis of what drives success in professional services firms that was nothing short of BRILLIANT! I still refer back to this model all the time and continue to use it on a daily basis."*

And the initiatives for creating opportunities to build a personal rapport came from both sides. Alex invited Cindy and her husband to a couple of the office functions at the law firm where he worked, while Cindy, for instance, arranged for her whole firm to go bowling with Alex one Friday after work. These events happened spontaneously, without prompting from either side.

- **Trust**

Trust had a lot to do with their success as well. Says Cindy:

"Alex did not hold back. He gave me access to his network and introduced me to people. He even referred some of his associates and friends to me, as clients. At the time, this almost ruined his relationships with those friends and associates, because D'bete Financials was just not ready to deal with clients of that calibre. But rather than seeing that as a negative, Alex used the opportunity to take the rather forthright feedback he received to assist me in identifying and fixing some fundamental process problems in my firm. And it was not all bad: we still have a very strong relationship with one of those clients, to this day.

"I believe that we both took (at least what we perceived to be) actual risks in going into this relationship, and we were both willing to put things that we truly cared about on the line. In a sense, I put my business

on the line, and he put his existing relationships with his friends and associates at risk. That, to me, is the very essence of trust and the foundation of our relationship today."

- **Supervision**

Finally, both Cindy and Alex believe that some form of supervision of mentorship relationships is probably not a bad thing. *"Every relationship goes through its ups and downs,"* believes Alex, *"and during the difficult times it helps if you are accountable to someone else for what you do."*

Of course, the *level* of supervision required in any particular relationship is something that must be determined in each instance. Alex was an unpaid volunteer, bound by little more than his passion and beliefs, and neither he nor Cindy would have faced any sanctions if they had failed to commit to the relationship. Alex recalls, *"Still, the involvement of The Nations Trust created an interesting dynamic, because there was always someone else to whom I was responsible, to whom I had made a commitment. And there was always a body that was willing and able to provide additional resources, skills and knowledge, if we had needed it."*

The financial records of D'bete Financials tell their own tale of this successful mentoring relationship. By September of 2005, cashflow was starting to improve, and amounts billed had risen noticeably. By July 2007, D'bete Financials was recording an increase of about 350 percent in amounts invoiced to clients, when compared to figures recorded in July 2005, while skills levels of staff had also increased considerably.

In early 2008, Cindy and Alex came to the decision that their mentorship relationship had run its course and was no longer required. This did not mean the end of their friendship, though, and they are currently planning a trip to the peak of Mt Kilimanjaro with a large group of friends.

❖ ❖ ❖ ❖

Mentoring to Retain Talent

by Adel Du Plessis

Adel Du Plessis discusses the ways and means for the new generation of young executives to gain the maximum benefit from mentoring relationships, by reviving the apprenticeship ethos.

Adel du Plessis qualified as a CA(SA) in 2001 at Deloitte Entrepreneurial Services & Corporate Tax. She lectured in Financial Accounting at Wits School of Accounting and Monash SA from 2003–2006. From 2007–2011 she explored entrepreneurship, coaching, teaching, writing and speaking on the "Softer Issues" in the CA(SA) profession. She is a founder and director of Lead for Africa (S21). She holds a Masters Degree in Accounting Education (cum laude)and has contributed to an international book on SA's education Challenges on the "Globalisation of Accounting Standards". Adel was a finalist for SACCI 2010 Business Woman, 1st Runner-up in 2009 for Mrs UN SA, and Silver award winner for ROCCI Community Services Champion. Her vision is to experience each day as she does her red wine – with all her senses! Adel can be contacted at adel@therapeia.co.za.

One of South Africa's tangible business challenges today is retaining scarce, *sought-after* talent, especially in Professional Service Firms (PSF). This is supported by an article, published in the January 2009 issue of the *Harvard Business Review (HBR)*, in which the authors argue that today's PSFs are so busy making money that they have lost the art of making talent. The *HBR* article studied more than 30 PSFs in depth, including consulting firms, accounting firms, investment banks, and universities. An interesting finding was that PSFs are becoming *corporatised* as they experience the burden of increasing competition and the necessity to grow rapidly in size and complexity.

The result is that mentoring for young professionals falls by the wayside because experienced professionals in some PSFs are assigned as many as 20 professionals to mentor, which leads to contractual relationships.

It is impossible for even the most people-orientated partners to develop professionals while continuing to execute their own business, manage projects, perform administrative functions, and even sometimes run special projects.

An evaporated mentoring culture is created, where young professionals begin to feel that they are merely cogs in a wheel. They feel alienated and see themselves as free agents, staying only until a better offer comes along. Other young professionals leave to maintain a work-life balance. We often hear young professionals complain that experienced professionals do not invest time in helping them to grow and develop.

I believe that in our developing country, where resources are scarce, the challenges for both experienced professionals (the mentors) and young professionals (the mentees) are here to stay. Enough has been said, done and developed to challenge and equip mentors to do their job in the workplace correctly.

Whether or not they are doing this is influenced by various factors, such as commitment, taking responsibility, available resources, adequate mentoring skills, and the time allocated for this work. In addition, we tend to neglect and forget the important role that the mentee has to play in this relationship, and what he or she needs to bring to the table. The responsibility, authority and commitment are not only the mentor's task – it is a two-way street.

Therefore, the important mature question with which I want to challenge our new generation is: "What can I do to reverse this damaging mentoring trend and ensure that my employer retains my talent?" The short answer: "Take the initiative and revive a traditional apprentice relationship with your mentor." The result is that if you take the action, you benefit from it. You learn from someone with vast experience, and you get it for free!

Basic principles to use as a guidepost in your new journey of mentoring/apprentice revival

It is very important to understand what it takes to build the basics of an apprentice relationship. One authentic characteristic of our South African culture is our ancestral apprentice relationships. I am sure that we can learn a lot from our grandparent's stories and tales on how the youngsters in a tribe had to learn from their masters in their apprentice relationships. I will give you basic principles to use as a guidepost in your new journey of mentoring/apprentice revival:

- **Mentoring is personal**

You need to feel comfortable with your mentor in all dimensions of your life. A mentor cannot be allocated to a mentee without consent from both parties, and most PSF Human Resources professionals support this. Therefore, if you do not feel comfortable with your current mentor, take responsibility and find someone to whom you can relate.

- **You need to ask the questions**

There is a misunderstanding in practice that the responsibility lies with the mentor to ask the questions. At Therapeia we feel strongly that it is the other way around. We have seen in our business that the best performers are those who ask questions and those who are not afraid to ask for feedback. Asking the right questions will result in getting the right answers to help you build your career.

- **Shadow your mentor**

In an authentic apprentice relationship, the apprentice observes the master's every move, action, words and behaviour to learn from him or her how things should be done. The master seldom asks questions, but sets the example through his or her actions. Therefore, you need to take responsibility for shadowing your mentor and observing all dimensions of his or her life.

- **Take initiative about getting together**

I have been in numerous discussions with young professionals as they voice their frustration with their mentor, who has not contacted them for a meeting. My simple answer is: "Why don't you contact your mentor and set up the meeting?" If I reflect back on my own journey, I have set up most of my mentor get-togethers. The result is that I get what I want, and the mentor admires me for my innovative action.

- **Reward your mentor**

We live in a consumer driven society where we expect to be served. Be different and serve your mentor for serving you! My experience is that the word *thank you* brings peace and healing and builds a relationship. In my mentor relationships, I have given mentors their favourite bottle of wine, spoiled them with coffee at a coffee shop, written them a thank you note, given them a voucher for a massage at a spa. It does not have to cost you a lot – do this once a year for your mentor and see what happens.

By applying these principles you will develop into a serving, wise young leader, mentoring your own peers on how to be a servant leader. Who knows, you may develop a new generation mentoring programme for your PSF. Through your initiative you ensure that your employer retains your talent, and because you developed it, you also get the best mentoring service.

❖ ❖ ❖ ❖

Why are Mentoring Programmes in South Africa Not Delivering?

by Penny Abbott and Peter Beck

Mentoring can be a highly-effective, affordable developmental tool that delivers amazing results. Penny Abbott and Peter Beck highlight six flaws found in many mentoring programmes and show us how to correct them.

Peter and Penny are founding Partners and Directors of Clutterbuck Associates South Africa, a leading consultancy in the support of organisations' coaching and mentoring programmes.

Peter Beck runs his own consulting business specialising in change and diversity and has recently added retirement living to his portfolio. He has a background as an HR practitioner with more than 12 years' operational/line experience and 18 years' organisational development with specific interest and experience in performance and change management, graduate and fast track development, discrimination management and management of diversity/relationship issues. He is active in the HIV/AIDS field in South Africa and has undertaken similar work in West and East Africa. He joined the University of Stellenbosch Business School as Faculty for the FNB Management Development Programme in 2010. He is a Chartered HR Practitioner Generalist, a Mentor with the SA Board for People Practice, and an Advisory Board member for the International Standards for Mentoring Programmes in Employment (ISMPE). He is a facilitator for Understanding Racism/Sexism/Classism and Developing Good Practice.

Penny Abbott uses her experience in management and leadership development, gained during her long and successful career in Human Resource Management, as the basis for her consultancy work in the field of coaching and mentoring. She has an MPhil from the University of Johannesburg in Human Resource Development and is engaged in doctoral research at the same institution. She is actively involved in Coaches and Mentors of South Africa and works on the Research & Definitions

Committee as well as leading the Mentoring Special Interest Group. She is a Master HR Practitioner and a Mentor with the SA Board for People Practice.

Contact them through http://www.mentoring.co.za/or at pbeck@ clutterbuckassociates.co.za or pabbott@clutterbuckassociates.co.za.

Mentoring is a required component of learnerships, social labour plans, industry BBBEE Codes, and professional development programmes. *King III* recommends mentoring for aspirant and new company directors.

Although it would appear that many, if not most, companies have mentoring programmes, this is not the case. We often find that discussions with companies regarding their mentoring programmes reveal one of the following scenarios:

* Their mentoring programme doesn't really work.

* It is not very widespread.

* Top management doesn't really support it.

* It's fading away.

Mentoring is not living up to expectations because of one or more fundamental flaws in programme design or implementation. In this article, we discuss these flaws under six headings, which are taken from the International Core Standards of the Standards for Mentoring Programmes in Employment (ISMPE)[1], endorsed some years ago by the European Mentoring and Coaching Council (EMCC)[2].

1. Clarity of purpose

There is a tendency for companies in South Africa, when faced with multiple requirements from government or industry sectors, to adopt a "tick box" approach to implementation of legislation and codes of good practice. Unfortunately, with mentoring, as with most other similar issues,

1   [Online] Available at http://www.ismpe.com/.
2   [Online] Available at http://www.ismpe.com/.

this simply does not produce a programme that delivers any real benefits to the organisation or to the participants. A good understanding of what mentoring can and cannot do is required, and from this understanding a proper business case can be built, which will justify the allocation of resources of attention, time and money to mentoring. Why should a busy manager spend time mentoring, if the business case is not clear to all concerned? Setting up a mentoring programme takes a lot of work and, usually, a long time.

Consideration of the business case for mentoring should be done, bearing in mind the many different objectives that mentoring programmes can be used, for example, for the following purposes:

- To learn to leverage diversity.

- To integrate people with disabilities.

- To on-board and accelerate the learning of newly-recruited graduates.

- To support learnerships.

- To accelerate development of high-potential managers in the succession plan.

Mentoring is likely to be most effective when it is closely integrated with other business and HR processes, for example, performance management, leadership development, career development, and diversity management. We find that basing mentoring discussions around the organisation's leadership competency model and a mentee's individual development plan ensures focus, gives a very clear line of sight, and delivers the best results for all stakeholders.

2. Stakeholder training and briefing

We often find that mentoring programmes are initiated within a Human Resources department, without significant consultation and buy-in from top management and other stakeholders, or that a management team has decided to implement mentoring without much discussion, and has completely delegated the implementation to the HR Department.

A mentoring programme is unlikely to work unless the top management team has had in-depth discussions about some of the difficulties and dilemmas that result from mentoring. One typical example is: what happens if the mentoring discussions result in the mentee deciding to leave the company?

There is very often confusion or lack of attention to clarifying the relationship between the mentor, the mentee, and the line manager. In one case, a manager thought that the job of the mentor was to help him "make the machine work", in other words, to bring a non-performer up to scratch. This confusion is exacerbated when there is confusion between what coaching is and what mentoring is. We find that it can be clarified if coaching and mentoring are explained as follows:

- Coaching refers to the creation of on-standard and excellent performance in the tasks of a job (the responsibility of a line manager or designated subject expert).

- Mentoring is allocated to an off-line, experienced person to help the mentee grow in his or her career, his or her professionalism and his or her deeper levels of competence, as in the definitions of the National Qualifications Framework, shown below.

Practical Competence	Demonstrates ability to perform a set of tasks.
Foundational Competence	Demonstrates understanding of what the performer is doing and why.
Reflexive Competence	Ability to integrate performance with understanding so as to show that the learner is able to adapt to changed circumstances appropriately and responsibly, and to explain the reason behind an action.

The critical stakeholders in a mentoring programme are the mentors and mentees. Yet, most often, they are not trained in mentoring skills. This results in mentees not understanding what mentoring is all about and how to take responsibility, and so they remain passive recipients in the mentoring process. Mentors also complain about mentees with a "victim mentality", or an "I want" attitude. The reality here is that this further reinforces the already serious levels of dependency and highlights the potential from the mentor's perspective of operating out of a defective thinking attitude.

We believe strongly that mentoring works when the mentee is empowered to drive the process. In order to do this, mentees need to be trained. When mentors are not trained, they tend to want to tell the mentee what to do and they dish out advice rather than helping the mentee to think through options and make decisions. Clearly, it's easier to tell the mentee what to do, yet this doesn't go down well with mentees from younger generations. This feeds into an issue many clients are grappling with of poor employee engagement and retention.

Mentors appreciate gaining an understanding through training of generational differences, for example, in the approach to work and to rewards. Training workshops for mentors and mentees work best when done on a modular basis and using a change-management approach, rather than a unit-standard-based generic training approach.

Many mentoring programmes struggle to find enough mentors, so they have to limit the number of mentees who could benefit from the programme. We find that organisations do not communicate and market the programme to potential mentors, highlighting why they should get involved, what is involved (for example, one hour a month for 12 months), and what the benefits to themselves would be.

3. Processes for selection and matching

Mentoring programmes usually have some criteria for choosing mentors and mentees, but often adopt a "similarity"-driven matching process, whereby mentors and mentees with a similar background or interest or experience are matched. This can help the pair to develop rapport, but can also result in mentoring sessions becoming too comfortable and not being challenging enough. Another problem is that mentees, when not trained and guided, like to choose as a mentor the most senior and/or influential person they know. This can lead to competition among the mentees and carries the danger of reverting to a sponsorship-driven relationship, rather than a developmental one.

One issue we often find is that organisations don't implement a small pilot programme first for six to 12 months. We recommend that a pilot programme should be restricted to about 10 mentoring pairs, and that it should then be evaluated with the mentors and mentees to see what may need to be adapted to work more effectively within the organisation's context.

4.   Processes for measurement and review

Measurement of outcomes of a mentoring programme is a complex topic, because mentoring will produce quite a few different outcomes. For example, a mentor may feel more satisfied in his or her job, because he has been passing on his experience to someone else. A mentee may feel more loyal to the company because of the mentoring programme. The leadership development programme may see an improvement in the leadership competency of developing others as a result of the mentoring activities of managers. Because of this complexity, and also because of misplaced concerns about not interfering in the confidential nature of the mentoring relationship, organisations often shy away from measuring whether the mentoring programme is working. This is un-business-like and undermines the likelihood that management teams will wish to continue a mentoring programme. If they can't see the results, why should they continue?

We recommend that an organisation adopt a model similar to the one below, which measure mentoring on several dimensions:

	Relationships	Scheme
Process	Measures specific to the scheme.	Measures specific to the scheme.
Outcomes	Measures specific to the scheme.	Measures specific to the scheme.

For example:

	Relationships	Scheme
Process	Both mentor and mentee are comfortable with the process.	Meetings are taking place as scheduled. Few re-matches.
Outcomes	Both mentor and mentee report achievement of objectives.	Improvement in leadership competencies of mentees. Improved retention of mentees.

5. Maintains high standards of ethics

Ethics in mentoring programmes include issues which should be discussed and published in a Code of Conduct, or Ground Rules, for the mentoring programme. These should cover items such as:

- The company will provide all parties in the mentoring scheme with a clear statement of scheme purpose and the behaviours expected.

- Mentoring is an inclusive empowering activity and the scheme coordinator will ensure that there is no discrimination – intended or unintended – in terms of gender, racial origin, culture, religion, or disability.

- The company will respect the confidentiality of the mentoring process, requiring feedback only with the consent of the participants.

- The mentee's line manager is entitled to be given an understanding of the scheme and its implications.

- Wherever possible, the company will provide mentees with a pool of mentors from among whom to choose, and guidance in how to make their choice.

We find that although organisations would like to have ethics such as these for their mentoring programmes, typically they have not thought through the content of such a set of Ground Rules, and therefore, the mentors and mentees don't have a clear framework within which to operate.

6. Administration and support

We know from research we have done in South Africa, which confirms results from overseas research, that the co-ordinator of a mentoring programme is absolutely central and critical to programme success and sustainability.

However, we often find that companies allocate the role of co-ordinator to someone who then leaves within 12 months or so, or who changes jobs and drops the role. The direct impact of this common occurrence is that mentoring becomes seen as the flavour of the month.

The co-ordinator's role is seen as administrative, instead of the organisation development role that it truly should be. Co-ordinators are often not aware of good practice in mentoring programmes and are most often not trained in the role. If the mentoring pairs are not monitored and supported, the mentoring relationships can falter and fail. It is critical for the co-ordinator to keep regular contact with the pairs and to have the skills to intervene if something is going wrong.

Mentoring can be a highly effective, affordable developmental tool which, if used in a well-designed and well-implemented mentoring programme, can deliver amazing results for all concerned. The six items discussed above should form the basis of all discussions and decisions on setting up a mentoring programme. A short PowerPoint® presentation summarising this article can be accessed on http://www.mentoring.co.za/.

❖ ❖ ❖ ❖

Wisdom from Professional HR Mentors: Transferring Knowledge from One Generation to the Next

by Marius Meyer

Based on the book, *Wisdom from HR Mentors*, Marius Meyer shares snippets of the individual and collective wisdom of 30 HR mentors. Learning from the wisdom and experience of these mentors, we can identify new ways for growing HR practice in our organisations.

> **Marius Meyer** is the CEO of the South African Board for People Practices (SABPP), the professional body for HR Management in South Africa (www.sabpp.co.za; contact Marius at marius@sabpp.co.za). He is also head of research for ASTD Global Network South Africa and an advisory board member for the Human Capital Institute (Africa). Marius is the author of 16 books and numerous articles.

Mentoring and coaching have grown significantly over the past ten years, both internationally and most certainly in South Africa – to such an extent that there have been hundreds of conferences and workshops on this important leadership development best practice. In particular, mentoring programmes have been used by many organisations to transfer wisdom from experienced leaders to newcomers, especially in professional occupations such as accounting, engineering, law, and human resources.

Based on the book, *Wisdom from HR Mentors*, this article reflects on the individual and collective wisdom of 30 HR mentors. Learning from the wisdom and experience of these mentors gives us the opportunities to indentify new ways for growing HR practice in our organisations. The mentors in this book are all part of the most prominent mentoring programme in South Africa – the South African Board for People Practices (SABPP).

The role of the SABPP

HR is a specialist profession with a pivotal role to play as caretaker of the most valued asset in business, namely people. If we fill the HR profession with practitioners who have scientific expertise and competence, together with a deeply-felt moral obligation to ethics and a duty to society, we will have done our country an inestimable service.

The SABPP has 144 mentors spread throughout South Africa, SADC and the Middle East. For decades, these mentors have built the HR profession by sharing their knowledge and experience with younger HR practitioners, and also advising the board of the SABPP on strategy and initiatives to enhance the HR profession.

They have been so successful in this effort that the South African Qualifications Authority has recognised SABPP as the professional body for HR and the official Education Training and Quality Assurer responsible for quality assurance of HR learning provision in South Africa.

Huma van Rensburg, CEO of SABPP, said that at the very heart of all professions are people "of good repute" who care deeply that their particular profession be practised with a sense of pride in excellence and who wish to protect the reputation of that profession. The 30 mentors of the SABPP have taken stock of their many years of experience and have highlighted the lessons they have learned.

A mentor is entrusted with the role of custodian of the professional standards laid down by SABPP and serves in an advisory capacity. The mentors are typically senior HR directors, consultants and academics. They become mentors by invitation because they are long-standing and committed senior registered Chartered or Master HR Practitioners.

Lessons from 30 HR mentors

What exactly did the HR mentors achieve? What can we learn from them and how can we use this information to inform future HR practice and professionalism? Here are some of the main lessons from the lives and work of the 30 HR mentors who all contributed to, *Wisdom from HR Mentors*:

- **All the mentors have emphasised the importance of education.** All of them completed at least an under-graduate qualification in HR management, while the majority of them have gone on to complete Honours and Master's degrees in HR management or a related discipline. Some of them have completed their doctoral degrees, and a handful of them are busy completing their doctoral qualifications.

- **The mentors believe in the importance of pursuing post-graduate studies as part of their career and professional development.** Interestingly, over and above their formal qualifications, the mentors have also benefited from relevant short courses in helping them to keep abreast of developments in the field. Thus, the mentors value education as a key component of their success.

- In addition to their academic studies, **all HR practitioners should actively become involved in continuous professional development** (CPD) as a formal way of developing themselves. SABPP's e-CPD process provides the platform for effective CPD.

- Given the fact that almost all the mentors are affiliated to other professional bodies or associations, it is clear that they have **all benefited from joining a network of like-minded professionals**. This has helped them to achieve excellence in the HR field, and to learn and network with fellow HR practitioners.

- The majority of the mentors, while being practitioners, are **actively involved in academic work**, either as assessors or moderators, or as authors and facilitators of learning sessions at universities or colleges. They have therefore not isolated themselves from the academic environment after their studies have been completed.

- Over and above their involvement in HR work, the **mentors have participated in professional development work for other organisations**, often not related to the domain of HR management, for example, churches and other community organisations. They, have therefore contributed to building a better society beyond the realms of the HR profession.

- The mentors have also **adapted to change throughout their careers**. For instance, some of the mentors are embracing social networking as powerful tools to transformation of the work and business environment. In an increasingly technologically-driven work environment, HR practitioners must become active participants in social networking opportunities and blogs to learn, network and share information.

- Instead of just studying case studies of companies as learning opportunities, universities and other training providers can use **individual cases of successful HR practitioners such as the thirty mentors to inspire students to learn about HR** and to prepare themselves adequately for the work environment. This approach of focusing on career-specific preparation is part of the new higher education and training landscape that has already been embraced by several universities. Using real-life mentors will reinforce and accelerate this approach to career-oriented teaching and learning.

- The mentors shared their views regarding **professionalism and the competencies needed to be effective as HR practitioners**. The most important competencies identified by the mentors were strategic partnering, leadership, communication, ethics, networking, change management and business acumen. HR practitioners should actively work towards building these competencies if they want to aspire to the highest possible level of professionalism.

- Learning from the personal visions from the mentors, **their overall message is about change**. Doing things in better and new ways will be critical for the future success of HR practitioners. However, HR practitioners will increasingly become strategic partners, but this time engaging with multiple stakeholders for the benefit of a

better society. A new virtual workplace will emerge and technology
will be key in this regard.

- To younger HR practitioners and newcomers to the HR field,
  their advice **register as an HR practitioner with SABPP and
  get yourself a mentor!** Liaise with the SABPP to enter a formal
  mentoring programme, or use mentoring opportunities offered by
  your organisation. One of SABPP's alliance partners, Coaches and
  Mentors South Africa (COMENSA), also provides valuable assistance
  with mentors and coaches throughout the country.

- The next decade will present an opportunity for **HR practitioners
  to address the gap between HR and the line of the business**. The
  HR–line interface is at the core of HR's credibility crisis. The ability
  of HR to bridge this gap will determine whether HR will arrive as
  a fully-fledged strategic partner in business.

For three decades, the SABPP has been the custodian of HR professional
standards in South Africa. The field has grown and developed into a
profession in which high level skills and competencies are needed. The
focus on ethics as a core competency shows that standards of ethical
conduct and behaviour are increasingly important in the workplace.
Likewise, a range of competencies is needed to be successful in this
dynamic and maturing field of HR management. Learning from the
lessons identified by the mentors and implementing the recommendations
outlined will further enrich the professional field of HR practice.

Setting standards for HR professionalism

HR mentors have empowered hundreds of more junior HR practitioners
who have grown and excelled in their careers – so much so that many
of them are now accomplished HR managers and consultants in their
own right. Thus, the wisdom from mentors has been passed on from
one generation to the next.

The real winners are not the mentors or the mentees, but the HR
profession. Over the last three decades, these mentors have shaped the

HR profession. Not only did they develop others, but they also set the standard for HR professionalism. They championed HR professionalism at organisations throughout the country and even across national borders. They implemented leading HR practices and represented people and business issues, championing the HR profession in the process. Many of them actively participated as speakers at conferences, seminars and workshops to build the HR profession; and they have written articles or books to share their knowledge and ideas with the broader HR and business market.

Contribution to the broader society

One of the most important elements of a profession is the contribution it makes to broader society. Just as lawyers are fighting for justice and the rule of law and order, HR practitioners have made a significant contribution to South African society.

HR practitioners were the first people to take ownership of the recommendations of the Wiehahn Commission in implementing fair work practices and labour laws in South Africa. Significant improvements in working conditions and conditions of employment were achieved in this way.

Significantly, the HR profession has embraced employment equity, and while most organisations in South Africa have not yet attained an equitable representation of designated groups throughout their companies, many HR departments have been totally transformed to reflect the composition of the broader South African society. It will not be a surprise if statistics show that HR departments are the first functions in organisations to have achieved employment equity targets.

It is important to realise that although HR mentors have made a significant contribution to the HR profession over the last thirty years, the new and emerging HR practitioners are entering the field in a totally different business and contextual environment, with its own realities and demands.

While certain key lessons as espoused by the mentors can most certainly be applied and transferred from one generation to the next, new challenges and complexities will emerge on the horizon. For instance, the power of technology, and the emergence of the virtual office and social networking in particular, will rewrite the rules of the HR game and level the playing field not only inside organisations, but also between job-seekers and employers, and across national boundaries and continents.

Thus, younger HR practitioners will be challenged to think through and outside the box, and should be able to reconfigure the HR world according to the demands of the times they are living in. When they replace this generation of mentors, they will impart their knowledge and skills to the next generation, and thereby become the new change agents in a radically different world.

Be that as it may, it all started with a cadre of senior HR mentors – professional people who put the HR profession first and ensured that they positioned and grew HR as a dynamic field of practice, consulting, and scientific study. In essence, while the industrial era was replaced by the knowledge and information era, leading HR mentors ensured that people became the heart of business.

I will conclude by using the words of one of the mentors and Executive Director of Corporate Services for the City of Cape Town: "In business, finance is referred to as the "bottom line". People, however, must be regarded as the top line."

❖ ❖ ❖ ❖

SECTION C

Coaching

- How to Select the Right Coach by **Cindy Bell**

- Enhancing Work Capacity with Coaching by **Samantha Stewart**

- External Coaching for Success by **Dale Williams**

- Coaching – Baking a Cake While Holding Up a Mirror to Yourself by **Karel van der Molen**

- Choosing an Executive Coach by **Natalie Witthuhn Cunningham**

- Coaching and Emotional Intelligence by **Kathy Bennett** and **Helen Minty**

- Coaching Strengths in a Weak Economy by **Dr Robert Biswas-Diener**

How to Select the Right Coach

by Cindy Bell

Coaching has been around informally for many years. As a new profession, it may be confusing to decide how to go about selecting a coach who is right for you and your particular needs, writes Cindy Bell. Here's how.

> **Cindy Bell**, the founder of Directions, is a talent management consultant that coaches and mentors individuals and business teams to focus their talent for profit.
>
> Cindy has over 25 years of business experience in the areas of marketing, advertising and talent management. Her studies in Communications, Marketing, various Business Best Practices, Thinking Skills, Education, Human Dynamics and Facilitation provide a foundation of reference.
>
> Cindy is an internationally accredited Meta Coach® and Trainer, and a Neuro-Semantics and NLP Master Practitioner, all of which are recognised by the International Society of Neuro-Semantics (ISNS).
>
> Cindy has a firm commitment to empowering people to take ownership and purposefully effect performance in their roles and responsibilities. Cindy can be contacted at www.careerdirections.co.za or cindy@careerdirections.co.za.

"In the last five years, coaching and mentoring have sprung to prominence in South Africa (SA). Because coaching and mentoring are relatively new, still-emerging disciplines in SA, a group of experienced business and life coaches initiated a discussion process in 2004 to facilitate the development and professionalisation of these fields. The result was Coaches and Mentors of South Africa (COMENSA) – the all inclusive, umbrella professional association for individual and corporate providers and buyers of coaching and mentoring services." – http://www.comensa.org.

This article not only adds credibility to this emerging profession, but also provides standards, frameworks and processes to ensure effective contracting and delivery of services. Taking personal responsibility for your coaching process from the beginning is the best strategy. The process outlined below would apply to individuals and companies needing a coaching project, as well as undergoing an accreditation process for preferred coaching suppliers.

A study by MetrixGlobal indicated a return on investment (ROI) of 529 percent for executive coaching. How can individuals and organisations successfully enjoy this powerful development process? Read on …

Some considerations

1. **Know what you want**

    - Explore the distinction between coaching and mentoring.

    - Check what is meant by coaching and whether it meets your needs.

    - Review some professional coaching body's frameworks (see, for example www.mcf.org).

    - Work out your personal or organisational goals which need coaching.

    - Assess your readiness for coaching.

2. **Know your criteria of assessment**

    - Determine what is important to you.

    - Determine what background, qualifications and certifications you require from the coach.

    - Do you need references and testimonials from existing clients?

    - How will the coaching needs analysis be undertaken?

    - Agree on the criteria for determining success.

    - Review how the coaches will tailor their methodologies to reach the required outcome.

- Agree on disclosure – confidentiality for the individual, and what details will need to be shared with their organisation, if any.

- Agree on the method and alignment with company requirements to be taken into consideration.

- Determine a code of ethics to adhere to.

3. **Know how the process will be driven**

- Identify and meet a selection of coaches (shortlist these by visiting websites, viewing listings of professional bodies, referrals, preliminary written applications, telephonic intro-interviews, and coaching trial session assessments).

- Know and ask your own tough questions.

- Assess your responses to your individual selection (rapport and understanding displayed by coach, inter-personal chemistry, subsequent feelings of empowerment, level of eagerness to commence).

- Be aware of the cultural fit for your organisation (observe coaching behaviour, and competence supporting your criteria).

- Confirm commitment.

- Clarify agreement (length of engagement, logistics, meeting venue, payment, face-to-face sessions, and whether it may take the form of, or include, telephone coaching, or a combination).

COMENSA defines coaching as "a professional, collaborative and outcomes-driven method of learning that seeks to develop an individual and raise self-awareness, so that he or she may achieve specific goals and perform at a more effective level". – http://www.comensa.org.

In SA, the founding organisation sponsoring MetaCoaching™ methodology development says that "while coaching is a conversation, coaching is not a warm and fuzzy chat. Nor is it teaching or telling people what to do. It is not even playing an expert in some content-specific domain. Coaching is about facilitating: through questioning, giving feedback, and running our own brains for more effective performance."

Coaching is distinct from other professional fields. So, if coaching doesn't advise and tell, what does it do?

Coaching:

- Is a facilitative process.

- Is a vigorous conversation.

- Asks high-level questions.

- Opens up possibilities.

- Holds a space for the client to become aware of solutions.

- Mobilises a client's resources.

- MetaCoaches do not let clients off the hook from what they want to do and who they want to be.

- Involves believing in the client's ability to maximise performance.

- Means taking on specific roles that facilitate implementation and actualisation for a client.

There are many categories of coaching, each of which focuses on a different aspect of development and may affect your selection of a coach:

- **Life/personal coaching** – the focus is on the individual's life, work/life balance, goals, career, purpose, etcetera.

- **Executive coaching** – involves leadership, management, vision and mission, grooming individuals for senior management positions, presentation skills, negotiation, career development, etcetera.

- **Internal coaching** – brings the best out of others as leaders and managers within an organisation.

- **Group or team coaching** – includes groups, group dynamics, teams, interpersonal relationships, organisational development, coaching for motivation, and buy-in contribution and productivity, etcetera.

- **Business coaching** – brings out the best of the business through skills enhancement in marketing, visioning, financial management, people management, interpersonal skills, time management, problem solving, creativity, and increased productivity.

Know your criteria of assessment

A key question in selecting a coach is whether the coaching relationship will serve the client. The coaching relationship is the critical vehicle that will contribute to the successful outcome of the coaching journey.

Three Cs for success

PeopleWise lives by the Socrates quote: "The unexamined life is not worth living". They are a provider that helps organisations to thrive through integrated leadership development and talent management, aligned with long-term vision and values. Furthermore, they believe that coaching requires three Cs for success:

- Chemistry
- Competence
- Commitment.

Firstly, the client should feel safe, but challenged, by the chemistry that develops between him- or herself and the coach. This is the key reason that clients engage in sample coaching sessions with a shortlist of coaches, before finalising their decision.

Secondly, the coach must be competent (in terms of training, skills and experience) and content (by focusing attention and effort on the client's growth, benefit and magnificence) to fulfil his or her various roles and actions in service of the client.

Thirdly, the relationship should engender commitment from both coach and client to "see things through" to the desired outcomes, by dealing honestly with the client's dreams, challenges and opportunities.

The required client commitment for coaching involves:

- Being ready to make changes in their lives

- Being ready to take responsibility for their coaching process

- Completing the tasks assigned and taking responsibility for the work agreed on during and between sessions

- Agreeing to be open, frank and honest.

Engaging a full-time professional coach

If someone tells you they have been a professional coach for over 20 years, start asking questions. Remember that coaching is not training, therapy, consulting or mentoring. Find out what their background is, and how dominant a role it plays in their coaching. Look for formal coaching qualifications and membership of local and international bodies COMENSA is a professional association not for gain, incorporated under section 21 of the Companies Act 61 of 1973, as amended. COMENSA is not just an association of providers, but is inclusive of all those providing or using these services.

How is COMENSA linked internationally?

COMENSA was encouraged in its founding years by I-Coach (Middlesex University London), the European Mentoring and Coaching Council (EMCC) and the Worldwide Association of Business Coaches (WABC). COMENSA is affiliated to the EMCC and WABC, and has taken part in the development of international coaching competencies for business coaches with the WABC. COMENSA members have spoken at international conferences for both organisations, and took part in the International Coaching Convention (ICC) held in July 2007 in New York, and the Dublin event in July 2008. The purpose of the ICC is to collaborate internationally to research, define and develop the coaching profession worldwide.

Evaluating professional competence

The COMENSA Standards Committee has drafted standards of professional competence (such as core competencies or skills) of a coach/mentor in five functional areas: questioning, listening, building rapport, delivering measurable results, and upholding ethical guidelines and professional standards. These are defined at four levels. The intention has been to devise criteria that are observable and measurable.

Coaching as a methodology is a great addition to the knowledge of any manager or supervisor who knows that the old "command and control" formal creates more resistance than solutions. Coaching as a leadership modality also recognises that leaders lead by mobilising and unleashing potential in people, through the framing of a vision and the embodiment of a story.

In the words of Albert Einstein, "We can't solve problems by using the same kind of thinking we used when we created them". Coaching in the business context empowers people to think differently; communicate more effectively; give and receive feedback more accurately; create structures of responsibility; become more empowered and accountable; and enable everybody in a group or team to work more efficiently. Concludes Buckminster Fuller, "You can't change anything by fighting it. You change something by making it obsolete through superior methods."

❖ ❖ ❖ ❖

Enhancing Work Capacity with Coaching

by Samantha Stewart

Like death and taxes, constant change is one of life's few certainties. The rate of change this century has increased exponentially, and the ability to adapt to change is now a critical factor in the survival of organisations. So how do organisations equip themselves to adapt to rapid change, writes Samantha Stewart.

Samantha Stewart is the holder of a BSC (Hons) and a BEd Adult Education (Hons). She started her working life as a microbiologist, moved onto HIV awareness and education, and then moved into the corporate world in the role of a Learning Consultant. Samantha is currently working as an independent learning and development consultant, is passionate about empowering people, and believes that coaching is one of the best tools to do this. She can be contact at sks@mweb.co.za.

In the book *The Dance of Change,* Senge (1999)[1] points out that many people in business incorrectly see learning and training as the same thing. They see training as a "frill, with no link to business results (or other desired results)". He goes on to contrast this with what he defines as the real meaning of learning. According to Senge, "to "learn" means to enhance capacity through experience gained by following a track or discipline. Learning always occurs over time and in "real-life" contexts, not in classrooms or training sessions."

So what does this have to do with organisations being able to adapt to the rapid pace of change in the 21st century? Simply put, in order to adapt employees need to be learning continuously and applying that learning to their performance. This is one of the key foundations of the concept of a learning organisation. Learning organisations promote the

---

1. Senge, P. 1999. "Orientation: Toward an Atlas of Organisational Change". In P Senge, A Kleiner, C Roberts, R Ross, G Roth and B Smith. *The Dance of Change.* London: Nicholas Brealey (p24).

concepts of learning and sharing in such a way, that the performance of all the individuals in the organisation benefits.

But why is Senge so sure that learning cannot happen in a classroom? For years, new employees were sent on numerous training courses to prepare them for the job and, when deemed competent against a number of learning outcomes, were then placed in the work environment and expected to perform. For some, this worked; however, for many, it soon became apparent that knowing and doing were not the same thing. The age-old cry of "we did not learn about that on our course" would be heard echoing down the corridors of the organisation. As a result, training departments were blamed for not doing a good job, and new vendors of training were sourced or new training programmes were developed, and employees would then be packed off for further training. There are a number of organisations that are still trapped in this way of thinking. We refer to this as the Training Paradigm.

The problem is that no matter how cleverly designed an experiential workshop may be, it is not the same as the working environment. That is not to say that there is no value in classroom work. The problem lies with the fact that this is often all there is. Once the classroom work is over, people are expected to perform back in the "real world", with little or no support. This is a little like expecting an inexperienced chef to cook a brilliant three-course meal, after having only read a recipe book!

If we apply Senge's approach to learning as something that occurs over time and in "real-life" situations, then we see that *real* learning occurs when the learner leaves the classroom and enters the workplace. However, this has certain risks attached to it. For example, I would certainly not be comfortable with a first-year medical student doing my medical examination. However, by the time a student qualifies as a GP, he or she has performed hundreds of medical examinations under the careful eye of a consultant. So the medical profession overcomes the risk of allowing a novice to perform in the "real world" by providing performance coaches. In business, the same must apply. If we follow

Senge's approach, then the role of trainer in the classroom must graduate to the role of performance coach in the workplace.

In an ideal world, dedicated performance coaches would be available to new incumbents to assist them in becoming competent in rapidly changing environments. In reality, however, this role falls to line management. So the challenge to modern organisations is to empower line managers to handle the role of performance coaches.

There are two distinct styles of performance coaching. Both are appropriate, but in different circumstances.

- **Performance management**

  Performance management is a role that enables performance by providing people with the required resources and stability to do their jobs. The focus is on rational structures and systems that co-ordinate energy and encourage the best contribution from everyone.

- **Performance leadership**

  Performance leadership is a role that inspires people to explore their full potential and to achieve performance beyond the ordinary. It engages people's inner selves and aligns organisational energy by focusing on the fundamentals – purpose, vision and values. This form of coaching is passionate about people and their potential contribution to a firm; the literature talks often of the "soul" of the leader.

When a new employee starts with an organisation, it is probably appropriate to manage him or her. However, as he or she becomes competent and able to perform, the line manager needs to make a shift towards more of a leadership style. Positive, proactive performance leadership is particularly needed to avoid our having to go too often down the slippery slope of disciplinary action and termination. This can be avoided by succeeding in leading people to explore their full potential and aspire to performing at their peak.

A tough question is why line managers so often seem to fail in the role of performance coach. A common observation is that line management is under such huge work pressure that they often find it difficult to balance the competing demands of world-class deliverables with employee learning and development. When surveyed, managers say that given the pressures under which they operate, they have real difficulty with three things:

1. **Pinpointing the reasons that a person is under-performing.** There is often no time to analyse performance. And, equally problematic, line managers often don't feel that they have an adequate framework with in which to identify all the factors impacting on performance.

2. **Giving people difficult feedback.** Managers feel that they lack the skills for giving difficult feedback. So they avoid it. Instead, staff find themselves bumped off projects as soon as their manager gets the chance to do so. But they don't know why, and if they are given a reason, it is often not the real one. This leaves both the staff member and the organisation unaware of their poor performance. There has been neither communication nor documentation.

3. **Experiencing difficulty changing from a management to a leadership style.** All projects, costs, processes and quality need tight management control. Unfortunately, it sometimes becomes difficult for managers to click out of control mode into the empowerment mode needed to lead experienced employees to perform.

Organisations that support their line management to overcome these difficulties are able to unleash the full potential of their personnel. In so doing they are able to learn and grow and thereby adapt to the changes with which they are challenged, in order to become ultimately a competitive force in their industry. Perhaps the real challenge is, who should performance coach the performance coach?

Unfortunately, there don't seem to be any easy answers to the difficulties that busy, stressed line managers experience in trying to become performance coaches for their people. But it's a problem, and it must be tackled by those organisations that passionately desire to be the best in their industry. Perhaps the way forward entails first engaging managers in analysing their problems and opportunities, and then providing them with performance coaches who can support the needed transformation. When people really get together to share and tackle their problems, solutions tend to be surprisingly plentiful.

❖ ❖ ❖ ❖

External Coaching for Success

by Dale Williams

Despite the current popularity of coaching skills, the value of external coaches to business has struggled for recognition. Dale Williams explains why.

Dale Williams has wide experience ranging from an executive level at Standard Chartered Bank to starting a business, which he later sold to a JSE listed company. Most recently he has headed up the Retail Bank for Standard Chartered in South Africa. Dale was selected to work on the International Secretariat based in Brussels, Belgium, and has travelled widely around the world. At the time, AIESEC members spanned 800 universities in 80 countries.

He was fortunate to be afforded the opportunity in 2002 to be in the pioneer group of a Masters Degree (MA) in Executive Coaching which was accredited through Middlesex University. This afforded Dale the opportunity to bring together his life experience and to build a model for Executive Coaching. During this time he created a methodology for using Scenario Planning in coaching, which he still uses as part of his coaching model. Commenting on this, Clem Sunter said, "*This is a unique application of the methodology of Scenario Planning; but the idea of looking at the future through a prism of possibilities is as relevant to an individual as to a business.*"

Updated information on Dale is available at his personal web site: http://www.connecteddale.com.

The 2007 British Chartered Institute of Personnel and Development (CIPD) annual survey on learning and development reveals some fascinating information – the survey shows that coaching has been completely integrated only into the wider field of HR, and learning and development strategy only within around 10 percent of respondents' companies.

Of even more significance is that proportionally more companies use line managers and internal coaches for coaching than they do external coaches. In cases where external coaches are employed, it is for less than 25 percent of the total work required. In fact, one in ten respondents to the survey say that it is line managers that make up more than 75 percent of the coaching activity taking place in their organisation.

Are external coaches missing the mark in terms of what they have to offer businesses? Will they ever be the major provider of coaching services within an organisation, or will this task always fall predominantly to internal coaches and managers? To understand this, we need to explore the dynamics behind choosing an external coach over an internal person.

In-sourcing vs outsourcing

The way that external coaches understand and integrate into an organisation is key to the role that they can play. As with any contract or outsourcing arrangement, the external coach and the company need to form a partnership to deliver the service. The strength of this partnership, and how it benefits the company, is of paramount importance to its success. This is important to understand, because it is the company that pays the bill.

In an outsourced arrangement, there are both pros and cons to using an outsider instead of an insider. Typically, organisations outsource so that they can focus on what they might call their "core competencies", namely the things they do best. Over the years, business has cycled between in-sourcing (doing it all ourselves) and outsourcing. When something new comes along – as coaching has over the past ten years – it needs to find its place within this cycle.

External coaches allow companies to focus on their "core competencies". A different style of management is required to ensure that the relationship is working and delivering the value that has been promised. For coaches to be successful, they need to understand this dynamic, and ensure that what they have to offer is competitive in relation to a company's in-sourced coaching options.

Coach remuneration

The cost of coaching is no doubt a factor affecting the adoption of external coaches. As a recent phenomenon, particularly in South Africa, the market has not yet established norms for coaching costs. Business coaching rates consequently vary widely from upwards of R5 000 per hour down to R500 or R600 per hour [in 2008 rands – Ed].

By comparison, the market for other contract professionals, such as project managers or business analysts, is fairly stable. Here, the market has sorted itself out based on factors that typically include qualification, and number of years of experience. With no widely-adopted standards available in the coaching industry, businesses find it more difficult to evaluate the return on their coaching investment.

For external coaches, not only the amounts but also the structure of charges vary widely. Some coaches charge up front; some take a percentage of salary; some lock people into long-term contracts; while yet others work on a pay-as-you-go basis.

These factors suggest, certainly from the buying side, a market that is not yet very sophisticated. This could be another reason why companies are more resistant to bringing in an outsider, while they remain comfortable working with internal coaches.

Roles and boundaries

The relationship that an external coach has with an individual client is very different from what an internal coach or manager can have. A large amount of the value of coaching is the powerful, honest, and often vulnerable conversation that takes place between coach and client. This happens partly because a person is a good coach, but also because the coach is an outsider. Someone who doesn't play a role in the business system where the client works can play a more independent role than an insider.

An executive position in a company is often a very lonely place to be. My experience is that the coach is often the sole confidant for executives, particularly when they face tough situations. The CEO of a company in particular, who is answerable to the board, is expected to deliver against agreed targets. This causes a dilemma if the CEO finds him- or herself in a place where he or she feels unsure about delivery. CEOs have their moments of doubt, just like everyone else. Who do they speak to in these moments? Would they speak to an internal coach? Likewise, further down the rankings in an organisation, would an executive speak to his or her manager about similar vulnerabilities? The way most businesses currently work, speaking about vulnerability is not broadly accepted.

Here, then, is the role of the coach – and, in particular, the external coach. Given the reasons above, it is unlikely that an internal coach will be able to have as much impact. The simple reason for this is that they are unlikely to establish as trusting a relationship as the external coach. The internal coach can play a role, but it will be limited when compared to the external coach.

In other parts of the organisation, away from the CEO and executive offices, an internal coach could possibly play more of a role. I would, however, contend that his or her agenda will always be questioned as a result of his or her being in the employ of the company, and not working independently of the business.

Manager as coach

Together with my partners, we've trained our managers in coaching skills. My experience of this work – in both a large multi-national and my own entrepreneurial business – is that coaching skills are undoubtedly an essential part of a manager's toolbox.

The ability to listen, understand, empathise and bring out the best in people is essential in business today. The era of "my way or the highway" has definitely passed. I would venture to say that managers who are not learning and using coaching skills have already been left behind. While these skills, labelled under the banner of "coaching", are fashionable in 2008, it does not mean that many managers understood previously that their job was to bring out the best in their team.

The difference, now, is that organisations believe that a manager can actually sit down and have a coaching session with one of his or her staff. This is entirely possible. However, those factors mentioned earlier will become a serious hindrance to the conversation moving beyond very safe and superficial topics. It takes a very special manager to create an environment where one of their staff could openly say, "I'm feeling really de-motivated because this company doesn't seem to have any leadership. I'm planning to leave but will hang out for my bonus at the end of the year." This is a fairly typical conversation held with an external coach.

Coaching skills for managers are powerful, relevant, and very effective in making them better at their jobs. These skills do not, however, make them coaches, and they will never be able to play the same role as an external coach.

The future

Looking back on the CIPD survey, it is interesting to note that despite the number of managers doing coaching, few respondents actually train their line managers to coach. Fifteen percent do not train any of their line managers to coach, while two thirds train only a minority. This trend is likely to change as more and more companies incorporate coaching skills within their training agendas. Managers seeking broader skills are also likely to find them incorporated within a number of other training interventions.

On the business side, I believe that more companies will look at coaching as they do any other procurement. It will quite quickly move away from being a special need, with managers afforded a large amount of discretion in whom they choose for and how they engage with coaching.

In a similar way to how companies manage other parts of their businesses, there will be standards and policies that will need to be conformed to. To be successful, external coaches will need to fit into the system created by the company, and will have to demonstrate real value in their offering. There are already models for measuring return on investment, and external coaches will need to be able to demonstrate the difference in the organisation as a result of their coaching.

The dynamic difference between internal and external coaches will continue. Just as companies pay top dollar for expert tax advice despite having internal tax specialists, so too will companies pay for really good coaches who offer demonstrable value.

A tool for measuring coaching's Return on Investment (ROI)

Coaching has been slow to demonstrate an ROI. The following example from the International Consortium for Coaching in Organizations (ICCO) illustrates one way of demonstrating this to your clients:

Value of resolving an issue	**Example** Avoided $65 000 in turnover costs Increased productivity by $45 000 Total benefit: $110 000
What percentage was attributable to coaching?	**Example** 50 percent attributable to coaching 50 percent of $110 000: $55 000
How confident are we of our estimates?	**Example** 80 percent confidence in our assessments 80 percent of $55 000 gives an adjusted coaching benefit of: $44 000
Subtract cost of coaching to get net benefit	**Example** Coaching cost $18 000 $44 000 less $18 000: $26 000
Calculate Return on Investment	**Example** Divide net benefit by coaching cost $26 000 divided by $18 000: 144 percent

Source: How coaching works – O'Connor & Lages (2007)

❖ ❖ ❖ ❖

Coaching – Baking a Cake While Holding Up a Mirror to Yourself

by Karel van der Molen

In this insightful article, Karel van der Molen explores the concept of coaching, its many benefits in helping others achieve peak performance, the qualities of a good coach, and the manager's role as coach.

Karel van der Molen is an extraordinary lecturer at the School of Public Management and Planning, Stellenbosch University.

He is an experienced human resource practitioner, coach and mentor, an admitted attorney, lecturer, facilitator, accredited trainer (ETDP SETA-accredited Assessor) and consultant with qualifications in law, financial services, and human resource management. He also has a strong background in all aspects of strategic and business management, people development and management, competency assessment, organisational transformation, and design high level of interpersonal interaction combined with sound problem- analysis capacity. Karel has well-developed communication, planning and organisational skills, with a strong aptitude for motivating and training teams and individuals in order to transfer skills. As well as having high levels of cognitive and emotional capacity, he is versatile, adaptable and energetic. He places strong focus on mentoring, empowering and enabling adult learners to become self-directed and life-long learners and to make an impact on their environments.

He can be contacted at email: kvdm@sun.ac.za or http://www.sopmp.sun.ac.za.

Introduction

South Africa, as a developing country, is experiencing all of the problems, challenges and opportunities associated with the very real shortage of relevant and appropriate human resource, technical and managerial skills, and this is having a decidedly negative effect on both the private and public sectors.

Organisations are faced with other dilemmas arising from the shortage of skilled employees. The issues relating to service delivery have in part been exacerbated by the ever-increasing lack of managers and other personnel. There is also the problem of experienced personnel who have accepted more senior positions in their organisations, or have accepted positions in other organisations being replaced with qualified, but inexperienced, staff. A third problem which occurs is when new, inexperienced personnel are appointed in an organisation.

We need to use a mixture of formal and informal approaches to ensure that the people-related short-, medium- and long-term goals of our organisations are addressed. One of these interventions, which can be utilised to deal with the lack of administrative, technical and managerial skills, is coaching.

Coaching and the coach – a definition or two

The term "coaching" appears to have its origins in the knowledge and skills required to control a horse-drawn carriage (Wikipedia, 2007)[1]. The word derives from the French word *coche* and derives originally from a small town in Hungary called Kòcs, where the first coach was built in the 16th century (Vickers & Bavister, 2005:17)[2].

As language evolves in the face of new technology (think of the impact of computer-speak in our lives today), it was not long before the noun "coach" became the verb "to coach", describing the transport of people from one place to another. And then, as language would have it, the term became part of the lexicon of English universities, describing a teacher or tutor who assisted or "carried" students through their studies and examinations.

From this foundation, it was not too long before the corporate world saw the benefit of coaching and embraced the concept as part of the

---

1 Wikipedia. 2007. Coaching. http://en.wikipedia.org/wiki/Coaching (Accessed 15 January 2007).

2 Vickers, A & Bavister, S. 2005. *Coaching*. London: Hodder Arnold.

management tools available to improve the knowledge, skills and competencies of employees at all levels of seniority within the organisation.

Noe (1999:241)[3] defines a coach as "a peer or manager who works with an employee to motivate him, help him develop skills, and provide reinforcement and feedback". Downey (2002:23)[4] describes a coach as a person who enables "the coachee to explore, to gain a better understanding, to become more aware and from that place to make a better decision that they would have made anyway".

Rogers (2004:7)[5] states that "the coach works with clients to achieve speedy, increased and sustainable effectiveness in their lives and careers through focused learning". Megginson and Clutterbuck (1995:4)[6] view the coach as someone who "shifts the focus to the results of the job; ... ownership is shared", while coaches are seen as people who are "motivated by helping their clients achieve their goals, deal with their issues, clarify what's them important to them – and a whole lot more" (Vickers & Bavister, 2005:10)[7].

Coaching – baking the cake

Coaching has often been equated with teaching someone to bake a cake. The mixing of the ingredients, the tips and good ideas to facilitate the learning of the novice baker, and then the joy as the cake is removed from the oven, iced and enjoyed are all, in essence, elements of the coaching process.

Chefs, cooks and bakers have something in common besides ability and the skills that allow them to rise to the top of their profession – and that special something is that each of them has a coach who is able to assist

---

3. Noe, RA. 1999. *Employee Training and Development.* Sydney: McGraw-Hill.

4. Downey, M. 2003. *Effective Coaching: Lessons from the Coach's Coach.* London: Texere.

5. Rogers, J. 2004. *Coaching Skills: A Handbook.* Maidenhead: Oxford University Press.

6. Megginson, D & Clutterbuck, D. 1995. *Mentoring in Action. A Practical Guide for Managers.* London: Kogan Page.

7. Vickers & Bavister, 10.

them to hone their natural abilities and skills, help them to achieve greater successes, plan ahead to meet future challenges and opportunities, and aid them to stay at their peak in the competitive industry in which they operate (Vickers & Bavister, 2005:17)[8]. This applies equally to individual chefs as it does to those working in teams in restaurants and hotels. These teams also have chief coaches, in addition to having specialist coaches who will concentrate on very specific skills and abilities that must be developed to ensure that the team gains the maximum benefit from the efforts of the individual team members (Vickers & Bavister, *supra*).

This parallel between the world of fine cuisine and the world of work is indeed relevant, given that one is looking to the skill of the coach to develop the chef and the employee in the workplace, both in the private as well as in the public sector.

The planning, leadership, organising, controlling and co-ordinating roles and responsibilities of a manager point to the fact that a good manager must also be a good coach (Meyer & Fourie, 2004:8)[9]. Coaching is an inherent part of the management process and should not be confined to annual performance reviews (Meyer & Fourie, 2004:13[10]; Vickers & Bavister, 2005:24[11]). Managers should be looking to the issues of identifying strengths and weaknesses, setting goals and objectives and assisting their staff in setting targets that will improve their overall performance in the work environment and, in so doing, lead to improved service delivery, greater innovation and enhanced performance.

Coaching is described as the "time-honoured way of helping others to achieve peak performance" (Foster & Seeker, 1997:1)[12]. Meyer and Fourie

---

8. Vickers & Bavister, 17.

9. Meyer, M & Fourie, L. 2004. *Mentoring and Coaching. Tools and Techniques for Implementation*. Randburg: Knowres Publishing (Pty) Ltd.

10. Meyer & Fourie, 13.

11. Vickers, A & Bavister, S. 2005. *Coaching*. London: Hodder Arnold.

12. Foster, B & Seeker, KR. 1997. *Coaching for Peak Employee Performance*. Irvin, (CA): Richard Chang Associates, Inc.

(2004:5)[13] provide a very comprehensive definition of the concept where they state that "coaching is the systematically planned and direct guidance of an individual or group of individuals by a coach to learn and develop specific skills that are applied and implemented in the workplace, and therefore translates directly to clearly defined performance outcomes that are achieved over a short period of time". It is also clear from the definitions given above that coaches provide assistance and guidance that is both proactive as well as reactive (Foster & Seeker, 1997:97)[14].

It can therefore be stated that coaching is clearly a shared responsibility, which corresponds to the statement by Downey (2003:23)[15] that the coach does "not direct, instruct or tell". Fleming and Taylor (2003:4) [16]state that coaching, "means *improving performance* at work, by turning *things people do* into learning situations, in a *planned* way, under *guidance*" (their emphasis) (see also Foster & Seeker, 1997:55)[17]. They further define coaching (*ibid.* 24) as "a process by which the coach creates relationships with others that makes it easier for them to learn". Zeus and Skiffington (2002:4)[18] state that coaching is about "exploring the individual's own values, vision and standards".

Coaching – holding up the mirror to yourself

It should be highlighted at this point that not every manager can or should be a coach. Many managers who are asked to coach their personnel are ill-prepared for this responsibility, and while they have all the necessary managerial and interpersonal skills, they lack the ability to

13. Meyer, M & Fourie, L. 2004. *Mentoring and Coaching. Tools and Techniques for Implementation.* Randburg: Knowres Publishing (Pty) Ltd.

14. Foster, B & Seeker, KR. 1997. *Coaching for Peak Employee Performance.* Irvin, (CA): Richard Chang Associates, Inc.

15. Downey, M. 2003. *Effective Coaching: Lessons from the Coach's Coach.* London: Texere.

16 Fleming, I. & Taylor, A.J.D. 2003. *Coaching Pocketbook.* Alresford, Hants: Management Pocketbooks..

17. Foster & Seeker, 55.

18. Zeus, P & Skiffington, S. 2002. *The Complete Guide to Coaching at Work.* Sydney: McGraw-Hill.

facilitate an improvement in the performance of the individual member of staff (Thompson, 2008:23)[19]. As the author states, "management is an assignment, and coaching is a choice".

There are also some individuals who feel that, "once a coach, always a coach". They feel that they can rely on their skills and abilities that taught competencies and brought success to protégés in the past, to achieve the same results as in the past. They utilise outmoded tools and techniques to coach the personnel and have not kept pace with the new methods and the changing world of work and the latest approaches to developing personnel.

It is, clear that the two instances noted in the preceding paragraphs can lead to a failed coaching process as the coaches have failed to look to their own growth and development. This is because they are not doing any self-evaluation and self-reflection – in other words, they have failed to hold up the mirror to take a cold, hard look at themselves and the manner in which they coach.

It is clear from the outset that one of the criteria for being a good coach is that he or she must "listen, ask questions, and enable coaches to discover for themselves what is right for them" (Rosinski, 2003:5)[20]. A coach must be self-motivated, good with people, and self-disciplined, in addition to having stamina and courage (Vickers & Bavister, 2005:4[21]; see also McDermott & Jago, 2005:134[22]). Vickers and Bavister (2005:11[23]) expand on these skills by highlighting the qualities of a good coach which they describe as:

---

19. Thompson, G. 2008. *Great Expectations: The Secret to Coaching*. CMA Management, April.

20. Rosinski, P. 2003. *Coaching Across Cultures: New Tools for Leveraging National, Corporate and Professional Differences*. London: Nicholas Brealey.

21. Vickers & Bavister, 4.

22. McDermott, I. & Jago, W. 2005. *The Coaching Bible: The Essential Handbook*. London: Piatkus Books.

23. Vickers and Bavister, 24.

- **Awareness and observation:** The coach should be aware of people as unique individuals with their own hopes, fears, dreams and aspirations. There must also be an awareness of the world and the environment in which the coach and the protégé live, work and function. (The author has used the word "protégé" in this article, but the word "coachee" is gaining more general acceptance.)

- **Curiosity and patience:** The coach should assist the protégé to explore and examine and question the issues that are important, which must be coupled with the ability to be a good listener (see also Fleming & Taylor, 2003:47[24]). The virtue of patience is equally important, as the protégé should and must do all the talking.

- **Empathy and building support:** An empathic approach shown by the coach allows a "space" for the protégé where he or she can speak and discuss issues freely, openly and honestly. This genuine concern and interest in the protégé will enable a connection to be made and a rapport to be created (also see Foster & Seeker, 1997:100[25]).

- **Respect, trust and integrity:** It is essential that in any coaching relationship an atmosphere is created where things that are promised are done and where there is confidentiality between the parties (Robertson, 2001:41[26]; Dove, 2006:24[27]; Stevens, 2008:82[28]).

- **Clarity of thought, confidence and approachability:** This is especially important when the protégé is confused and seeks answers, needs the assurance of a confident coach, and is comfortable in approaching the coach for assistance.

---

24. Fleming & Taylor, 47.

25. Foster & Seeker, 100.

26. Robertson, SJ. 2001. "An Effective Coaching Relationship for Managers." University of Witwatersrand: Unpublished Master's thesis submitted to the Faculty of Management.

27. Dove, JT. 2006. "Establishing Effective Organisational Coaching Strategies." Nelson Mandela Metropolitan University: Unpublished Master's thesis submitted to the Faculty of Business and Economic Sciences

28. Stevens, N. 2008. *Learning to Coach*. Oxford: How To Books Ltd.

- **Solution-focus and detachment:** One of the crucial qualities that a coach requires is that he or she must constantly look to solutions, rather than dwelling on the past and what may have gone wrong in a situation. It is also essential that the coach should remain detached and objective when the issues that are important to the protégé are being discussed.

- **Positivity and creativity:** These qualities are essential, as they will "rub off" onto the protégé and will encourage a different approach to dealing with issues.

- **Challenging, honesty and encouragement:** It is important for the coach to challenge the protégé to give of his or her best and also to be open and honest and direct with feedback in his or her discussions. The coach should also have the ability to encourage the protégé to move outside his or her comfort zone and to try something new and challenging.

- **Compassion, open-mindedness and admiration:** The coach must be able to work with a protégé with tolerance, without any prejudice or pre-conceived ideas. It is essential that the coach should view the protégé as someone with very special qualities that he or she, as the coach, will be able to assist in developing to their full potential.

- **Relaxed-approach:** A relaxed and even-tempered approach by the coach will assist the protégé when he or she is required to consider different and creative solutions to issues.

- **Self-awareness:** The coach should have the ability to reflect on experiences in order to enrich the experience of the protégé.

- **Authenticity:** It is essential that coaches should be real and authentic and not feel that they should be acting a part. They are in the first instance human beings and only thereafter coaches.

One of the questions that is frequently asked is whether the coach should be an expert in his or her field. This important issue is dealt with in an article in the *Harvard Business Review* (July–August 2007) where the authors (Ericsson *et al*, 2007:115[29]) state that rigorous research has shown that it will take up to a decade for an individual to gain expertise in a particular field and that the person will need to "[engage] in "deliberate" practice – practice that focuses on tasks beyond [his/her] level of competence and comfort." This has then led to the conclusion that *"experts are always made, not born"* (their italics). This then leads one to say that it is important that the coach should be looking to build on his or her abilities and would also benefit from acquiring a well-informed coach to assist him or her in becoming adept at the new skills and competencies, and also to become an even better coach.

A coach must have the ability to encourage others to go beyond their current level of performance (Foster & Seeker, 1997:9[30]; Robertson, 2001:29[31]) and should have some very special attributes, which can be described as:

- Wanting to share knowledge and experience

- A willingness to invest the time for the protégés and the organisation

- A belief that personnel are capable of an improved performance

- Not expecting to take credit for the improvement in others

- Enjoying working with people (Fleming & Taylor, 2003:17[32]; Robertson, 2001:31[33]).

Coaching – a final word

One of the realities of the workplace today is that the pace of change requires a manager to produce results more quickly than was the case in the past. It is equally clear that the traditional methods of management (for example, organising and controlling) are no longer effective today,

29. Ericsson, KA, Prietula, MJ & Cokely, ET. 2007. The Making of an Expert. *Harvard Business Review*, 115, July–August.

30. Foster & Seeker, 9.

31. Robertson, 29.

32. Fleming & Taylor, 17.

33. Robertson, 31

as personnel respond and react far better to reward and recognition for their work.

There is a paradox in the manner in which managers manage their time: in order to create more time for themselves to attend to their duties and responsibilities, they must invest time in the development of their personnel and, it must be said, of themselves. Sheppard *et al* (2006:3) state the purpose of coaching as a management competency when they say: "Ultimately, coaching others makes your life as a manager easier". This can be rephrased by saying: "Ultimately, self-contemplation and being a coach makes your life as a manager easier."

References

Dove, JT. 2006. "Establishing Effective Organisational Coaching Strategies." Nelson Mandela Metropolitan University: Unpublished Master's thesis submitted to the Faculty of Business and Economic Sciences.

Downey, M. 2003. *Effective Coaching: Lessons from the Coach's Coach.* London: Texere.

Ericsson, KA, Prietula, MJ & Cokely, ET. 2007. The Making of an Expert. *Harvard Business Review*, 115, July–August.

Fleming, I. & Taylor, AJD. 2003. *Coaching Pocketbook.* Alresford, Hants: Management Pocketbooks.

Foster, B & Seeker, KR. 1997. *Coaching for Peak Employee Performance.* Irvin, (CA): Richard Chang Associates, Inc.

McDermott, I. & Jago, W. 2005. *The Coaching Bible: The Essential Handbook.* London: Piatkus Books.

Megginson, D & Clutterbuck, D. 1995. *Mentoring in Action. A Practical Guide for Managers.* London: Kogan Page.

Meyer, M & Fourie, L. 2004. *Mentoring and Coaching. Tools and Techniques for Implementation.* Randburg: Knowres Publishing (Pty) Ltd.

Noe, RA. 1999. *Employee Training and Development.* Sydney: McGraw-Hill.

Robertson, SJ. 2001. "An Effective Coaching Relationship for Managers." University of Witwatersrand: Unpublished Master's thesis submitted to the Faculty of Management.

Rogers, J. 2004. *Coaching Skills: A Handbook.* Maidenhead: Oxford University Press.

Rosinski, P. 2003. *Coaching Across Cultures: New Tools for Leveraging National, Corporate and Professional Differences.* London: Nicholas Brealey.

Stevens, N. 2008. *Learning to Coach.* Oxford: How To Books Ltd.

Thompson, G. 2008. *Great Expectations: The Secret to Coaching.* CMA Management, April.

Vickers, A & Bavister, S. 2005. *Coaching.* London: Hodder Arnold.

Wikipedia. 2007. Coaching. http://en.wikipedia.org/wiki/Coaching (Accessed 15 January 2007).

Zeus, P & Skiffington, S. 2002. *The Complete Guide to Coaching at Work.* Sydney: McGraw-Hill.

❖ ❖ ❖ ❖

Choosing an Executive Coach

by Natalie Witthuhn Cunningham

Natalie Witthuhn Cunningham feels that action is needed to winnow out bad and ineffectual coaches. One way to assist in developing credibility for the profession is for the end users (the clients and organisations) to be rigorous in their selection process of coaches. Charlatans would then be weeded out. Nevertheless, the sole responsibility should not rest with the users of coaching services – it is the emerging profession that needs to be responsible for developing codes of ethics, and so on for its peers.

> **Natalie Witthuhn Cunningham** is Director of the Origo Consultants – a coaching and organisational development consultancy which has been in existence for 20 years. Natalie was recently Director of the Leadership Development Centre at Wits Business School. She was also instrumental in developing a Masters in Management in Business and Executive Coaching, as well as setting up a Coaching Supervision Certificate and Business Executive Coaching Certificate. She also headed up all the coaching in support of Leadership Development Programmes at Wits. She holds a BA (SW) Hons and an MBA from Wits. She is currently conducting her PhD research on "Identification of the Constructs of Business and Executive Coaching". She was a founder member of The Coaching Forum – a supportive thought leadership forum for independent coaches. She attended the Global Coaching Convention in Dublin, Ireland in 2008 which resulted in the Dublin Declaration on Coaching (now signed by 15 000 coaches worldwide). She is also one of 30 international experts who sat on the Worldwide Association of Coaches (WABC) committee to determine competencies of coaching. She sits on the Board of Graduate School Alliance Executive Coaching (GSAEC). She can be reached at Natalie.witthuhn@wits.ac.za or on 011 717 3550.

The Coaching Industry has grown rapidly in the last five years. The global coaching industry was estimated to be a two billion dollar per annum market in 2006 (Fillery, Travis and Lane, 2006). The Chartered Institute of Personnel and Development in the UK (CIPD, 2006:2) reported that 79 per cent of survey respondents are using coaching within their organisation and that 77 per cent say that coaching has been increasing in recent years. No current research exists for South Africa, but the trend would follow the same pattern. As the *Harvard Business Review* (HBR) research article on Coaching in January 2009 states; "Coaching exists to help executives find solutions, yet the field of coaching must solve a few problems itself. Coaching as a process is highly effective, but the field feels as if it is in its *adolescence*." Many coaches are concerned that a lack of entry barriers leaves the profession vulnerable to being discredited by charlatans. At present, the reality is that as long as inexperienced, unskilled people continue to be appointed as coaches, it remains increasingly difficult to professionalise the industry. The question for end users of coaching is: How do you select the ideal coach? Who is the best coach? What criteria do you use when selecting a coach? Many organisations are beginning to set up rigorous screening processes in the selection of coaches, but this is in its infancy, not only in South Africa, but worldwide. The purpose of this article is to provide some guidelines in the selection of coaches.

Executive readiness

Firstly, ensure that the willingness and readiness of the individual who is about to embark upon the coaching, is real and deep. He or she must want to be coached. All the research and empirical studies show this. Coaching is not an intervention for remedial purposes. It should not be used to address a problematic issue that should be addressed through other mechanisms such as disciplinary enquiries. Coaching is most effective when used to develop the capabilities and potential of individuals. Its focus should be enhancement of skills as opposed to addressing specific derailing behaviours. While part of the coaching process may explore derailers, this should not be the prime motive for coaching.

The executive should be allowed to choose his or her own coach. There are many methods of achieving this selection. Some coaching providers have chemistry sessions between the executive and a few coaches. Others even make coaching selections based on dating principles. Some have a group of coaches in a room where prospective executives/clients are able to spend ten minutes with each coach and question him. After an hour they select which coach they would prefer.

At the Leadership Development Centre of Wits Business School, we find executives are too busy for these processes. The process we follow is to ask the executive some questions through a written e-mailed questionnaire. These cover some demographics such as preferences and/or issues regarding race, gender and age, for example, and also what the client is looking for from the coaching process. Questionnaires are confidential. We then process the information and from our database of coaches select three résumés in which the coaches state their coaching philosophies and approaches in their own words. This allows the executive to get a feel for each coach. They then select one, and a meeting is set up. This shortlist of three coaches is compiled by our expert team and is based on the completed questionnaire. While executives have the right to choose a second meeting with a different coach, in our experience this has never proved to be necessary. But it is important that whichever process is followed, the executive has the right to accept or decline the chosen coach.

Experience and references

P Anne Scoular, a global provider of training for executive coaches (who also teaches coaching at London Business School in England), commenting on the January 2009 HBR Coaching Research report, said: "The surveyed coaches agreed for the most part that companies need to look for someone who has had experience coaching in a similar situation but hasn't necessarily worked in that setting. Organisations should also take into account whether the coach has a clear methodology. Although experience and clear methodologies are important, the best credential is a satisfied customer. A full 50 percent of the coaches in the survey indicated that businesses select them on the basis of personal references. So before you sign on the dotted line with a coach, make sure you talk to a few people she has coached before." (*Harvard Business Review*, 31 January 2009, www.hbr.org). Malcolm Gladwell, in his 2008 book

Outliers, introduces us to the 10 000-hour rule. The idea is that you have to practice something for 10 000 hours to master it. That's about ten years of practice. So mastery is impossible without an investment of ten years, which combats the idea that talent is something people have or don't have. It takes investment to achieve mastery. Does the coach you select have the 10 000 hours or a significant proportion of those hours?

Qualifications of coaching professionals

This is a difficult area as there are many qualifications in coaching ranging from a four-day course to doctorates. There are also many institutions offering qualifications, as the industry is not currently regulated. Anyone may offer a qualification. This makes it difficult for the client to discern the quality of the training received. One of the key factors clients need to explore is the credibility of the institution offering the qualification, the alliances of that institution to professional coaching bodies, and, a possible further factor, the methodology of the institution. Does it teach only one methodology or several? Coaching is a multi-disciplinary profession and the eclectic nature of coaching should be represented within the educational and development framework of the training institution's approach. If an executive is considering coaching, he or she needs to ask what business knowledge the prospective coach has and where this knowledge was obtained. There are a variety of professional bodies (from the locally-based Coaching and Mentoring Association of South Africa [COMENSA] to the international Internal Communicators Forum [ICF] to the American-based Worldwide Association of Business Coaches [WABC]) each of which has a different emphasis, although all are considered reputable and credible bodies. When interviewing a coach you need to ask of which professional bodies they are members or are affiliated with. You also need to know that your coach is aware of what is happening in the coaching industry and is not operating in a vacuum.

Anthony M Grant (anthonyg@psych.usyd.edu.au) is the founder and director of the Coaching Psychology Unit at the University of Sydney in Australia and he states: "Given that some executives will have mental health problems, firms should require that coaches have some training in mental health issues – for example, an understanding of when to refer clients to professional therapists for help. Indeed, businesses that do not demand such training in the coaches they hire are failing to meet their ethical obligation to care for their executives." (January 2009/Harvard Business Review 32).

Conclusion

While this is not an exclusive and exhaustive article on the subject, it does address the process of screening and selecting, and in so doing begins to ensure that the investment in coaching will get its return and that a meaningful process with meaningful results will be achieved.

❖ ❖ ❖ ❖

Coaching and Emotional Intelligence

by Kathy Bennett and Helen Minty

Kathy Bennet and Helen Minty discuss the benefits of coaching and its role in building peoples' emotional intelligence and enhancing their personal and work-related life performance.

Kathy Bennett has had extensive experience in Human Resource Management in the pharmaceutical industry. She has established herself as an independent Organisation Development consultant and has expanded her offering to include coaching – providing leadership coaching and leader-as-coach development to organisations. She has recently commenced with her doctoral studies in leadership with the University of Johannesburg. She is a faculty member of the business school of the University of Stellenbosch (USB-ED), and is involved in their Certificate and Masters (MPhil) coaching programmes.

Helen Minty's passion lies in partnering people to reach their full potential, facilitating them to perform more effectively in their workplaces and to achieve a greater sense of fulfilment as individuals. She has been involved in people development for more than 20 years, as a Training Manager, as a Training Consultant, and currently a Business Coach. Helen believes in the importance of Self-Leadership and Emotional Intelligence, not only for people to be personally successful, but also as prerequisites for the effective leadership of others. She supports individuals and groups in creating more engagement with both work and life, so as to become the very best they can be. As a life-long horse riding enthusiast, Helen also uses horses to promote Emotional Intelligence. Helen has a Post-Graduate Diploma in Management from Wits Business School, is a Neuro-linguistic Programming Master Practitioner and a certified Meta-Coach, and holds a Masters in Professional Coaching through Middlesex University (UK).

Kathy and Helen can be contacted respectively at kbennett@global.co.za and helenlsd@mweb.co.za.

In the business world, it is often said that you may be hired for your Intelligence Quotient (IQ), but if you are fired it is likely to be because of your lack of Emotional Quotient (EQ) or emotional intelligence. We know that success cannot be predicted by IQ alone, because in spite of high IQ, some individuals do not fare well in life. Others with more modest IQs do surprisingly well. Daniel Goleman asserts in his book *Working With Emotional Intelligence*, that emotional intelligence at work matters twice as much as cognitive ability or technical expertise. Unlike IQ, which is genetically determined and therefore fixed, emotional intelligence can be developed. Organisations are recognising the imperative both to create more star performers, and also to improve the performance of those who are floundering, through enhancing EQ.

The case for EQ coaching

Typically, organisations seek to enhance emotional intelligence through training courses. This is obviously designed to provide the greatest impact at the most reasonable cost. And with many individuals who attend such training, this objective is achieved. In some instances, however, training fails to deliver improved results. While there may be many reasons for this, appropriate development options need to be selected, bearing in mind individual needs. For some people, coaching provides a valuable supplementary process, or it may be an alternative to training, for example, when emotional intelligence issues negatively affect a person's current performance or stand in the way of promotion. Executives also often prefer the privacy that coaching offers.

The most important contribution of coaching is that it is carried out one-on-one which allows both coach and coachee to focus specifically on problematic issues. The level of trust generated in an effective coaching relationship encourages frank dialogue and allows objective evaluation of the gaps between actual and required competence. Coaching is not therapy, although it may require reflection on past behaviour; the goal of coaching is to enable effective future performance. Coaches are trained to refer those who need additional professional assistance to appropriate therapists.

This article discusses five issues to consider when deciding whether coaching can contribute meaningfully to the development of emotional intelligence.

1. Poor self awareness

Assessing our own emotional competence is fraught with pitfalls. Many of us over-rate ourselves. We may not want to appear incompetent or bad to others. We may quite naturally want to believe we are more capable than we are in reality. And if we lack self-awareness (one of the important dimensions of emotional intelligence), how can we be trusted to be objective about our own strengths and weaknesses? If we sit at an executive level, we may fall prey to the belief that due to our success, we have no real weaknesses.

The coaching contribution

Where you suspect that a person has poor self-awareness, coaching can be pivotal in preparing that individual for change. Through questioning techniques, coaches guide people towards recognising their own self-deception, creating awareness of differences between perception and reality. Coaches listen closely to uncover limiting beliefs. They reflect them back to coachees and then assist in changing these into empowering beliefs that support increased emotional competence. Coaches direct people to reflect on past work-related incidents and so to notice what they had not noticed at the time.

Assignments for creating awareness are a key focus of coaching. These may involve personal reflection, collecting feedback from others, putting actions into practice, noticing results and then looking for patterns in behaviour. Susan Ennis, head of executive development at Bank Boston told Daniel Goleman: "When self evaluation is purely between you and your coach (confidential, not seen or kept by your company) then you'll be more candid, or as candid as you can be, given whatever other limit you may have on self-awareness."

2. **The 360-degree assessment**

EQ training programme delegates are often evaluated by others, usually through a 360-degree assessment process. These assessments are often useful in supporting delegates' self-perceptions. They may also be useful in revealing delegates' blind spots and therefore act as a powerful stimulus for change; although they typically show average scores only. The delegate may not be given insight into the scoring patterns which create the average scores she sees. Assessments are generally carried out only at the beginning of training programmes. This means that neither the delegate nor his manager has any objective measurement of where or how he may have changed as a result of training.

The coaching contribution

Where a person's emotional behaviour is critical to their performance or is creating specific problems in the work environment, coaching can be a valuable supplement to a training. Coaches examine scoring patterns with the coachee, noticing trends and anomalies. They question the reasons for these and assist people to recognise specifically the behaviours that have created them. The coachee is directed to draw up action plans to address areas needing improvement. Putting these action plans into practice becomes an important focus of the coaching process. Coaches carry out post-coaching assessments. Results are examined as above and fed back to the coacheee and her manager. This provides a clear indication of where change has taken place and what still needs to be worked on.

3. **Change**

If we are, or choose to be, oblivious of the need to change, we will resist any encouragement to behave differently. Sometimes, through training, although we may become more aware of a need to change, we are still not able to make the actual decision to implement this change. We may simply think about it or talk about it and fall short of action. Some people spend years telling themselves that one day they will change. At other times, through training, we may try half-heartedly to change, but if our attempts are thwarted, we are likely to give up and go back to previous behavioural patterns. Only those who are really ready to focus on how to behave more effectively will benefit from training, provided it offers them an opportunity to develop a plan of action.

The coaching contribution

If you believe a person is unwilling or unable to make changes to emotional capabilities, it would be important to include coaching as part of EQ development. Coaches assist people to change by creating an understanding of the personal value of change. They enhance motivation and stimulate the individual to make a concrete decision to behave differently. Coaches assist coachees to identify not only what needs to be done differently but also how it needs to be done. This includes changing thinking patterns, tone of voice, words used, and body posture in order to introduce and/or establish an integrated and in-depth pattern of new behaviour for the coachee to follow.

4. Behaviour gaps

Altering habits requires practice. If there is a large gap between a person's current and desired behaviour, it is often difficult to put new behaviours into practice after training. Someone with a moderate degree of social skill may readily learn how to retain composure when dealing with a difficult customer, for example, because this requires building on a competence they already have. For someone with poor social skills, however, the challenge to listen and be empathetic in the face of someone else's rage may be overwhelming.

The coaching contribution

Where there is a big difference between emotional competence before training and what is required in the workplace, coaching might be a valuable addition to training. Through ongoing supported practice over a period of time, emotional competence is progressively developed. Coaches set small targets initially that can be built upon with time and increasing expertise. Coaches assist coachees in various ways to prepare for challenging situations, including through mental rehearsal. As candidates put action plans into practice, they behave differently and so begin to alter thinking patterns.

Coaches are personal cheerleaders. They offer non-judgemental support, whether people succeed or fail. They encourage them to examine what worked well and why, as well as what did not work well and what they need to do differently next time. They create enthusiasm for facing and overcoming obstacles.

5. Personal self-confidence

When someone struggles to change attitudes or beliefs after training, the amount and success of practice (how much they need to do and how successful they are) is dependent on sufficient self-confidence. Self-confidence is an important component of emotional intelligence. Given at least an average level of confidence, people are usually capable of putting tentative new behaviours into practice. If they achieve success, they will be encouraged to continue. If at first they don't succeed, hopefully they will try and try again. But what of those people who lack self-confidence? What are the chances that they (regardless of their belief in the importance of change) will have the courage to practise? Or if they do practice and are not successful, what are the chances that they will try again? And then having recognised even more clearly the gap between what they can do and what they ought to be able to do, what are the chances that their self-confidence will not be further eroded?

The coaching contribution

Where self-confidence is an issue for someone trying to improve emotional competence, coaching provides critical support. This is not only in terms of the practice of new behaviours but also in developing confidence itself. Coaches nurture self-confidence. Emphasis is placed on learning (both from successes and failures) and a recognition that competence increases incrementally. This minimises the emotional cost of not getting it right, especially early in the process of change. Ongoing dialogue directs behaviour towards increasingly successful outcomes and gradually builds the self-efficacy that promotes confidence and belief in oneself.

Conclusion

Training programmes that include sufficient practice and the development of action plans will enhance the emotional intelligence of many individuals. These include those who realise the value of change and those who already have a reasonable foundation of EQ upon which to build increased competence. Training is useful for those whose workplace EQ is neither critical to their performance, nor problematic. In deciding to supplement EQ training with coaching, you need to consider the following:

- Is this person's continued employment or career dependent on enhanced EQ?

- Does this person lack overall EQ competence in a specific critical area?

- Is this person a senior manager or executive who would prefer confidentiality?

- Does this person have seriously poor self-awareness?

- Does this person significantly lack self-confidence or self-esteem?

- Is this person unwilling to change?

- Is there a substantial gap between actual and required EQ competence?

- Is there a need to measure progress in the development of EQ over time?

The value of coaching is that it provides longer term opportunities for developing emotional intelligence, especially where short-duration training alone will be insufficient. In addition, it increases the sustainability of behavioural change because it supports the gradual development of integrated new habits and thinking patterns. Coaching therefore clears the roadblocks that disable performance. Coaching unlocks hidden potential and opens the way forward for personal and career growth.

❖ ❖ ❖ ❖

Coaching Strengths in a Weak Economy

by Dr Robert Biswas-Diener

With clients on the lookout for approaches that will produce the best results with the smallest possible capital expenditure, it is a great time for those who use strengths-based coaching approaches. In this article, Robert Biswas-Diener introduces us to the strengths approach to coaching and educates us about some of the related background research. He goes on to explain some practical strategies for using this information in your own practice or organisation.

Dr Robert Biswas-Diener is widely known as the Indiana Jones of Positive Psychology because his research on happiness has taken him to such far-flung places as Greenland, India and Kenya. He is a part-time instructor at Portland State University and sits on the editorial boards of the *Journal of Happiness Studies* and the *Journal of Positive Psychology*. Robert is a Certified Mentor Coach (CMC) and has worked with clients on four continents. He is author of *Practicing Positive Psychology Coaching* (2010), *Happiness: Unlocking the Mysteries of Psychological Wealth* (2008) and *Positive Psychology Coaching* (2007). He is also co-founder of the Charitable Mission. He is a coach, researcher and Programme Director at the Centre for Applied Positive Psychology (CAPP). Learn more about him at http://www.intentionalhappiness.com/ or http://www.cappeu.org.

We are experiencing a unique moment in economic history. Dramatic changes in the global housing, petroleum and currency markets have resulted in a sustained international economic downturn. In some of the most dramatic cases, national banks are failing, as in Iceland, or unemployment is creeping steadily upwards, as in the United States. Coaches, managers and others who serve organisational personnel find themselves in a unique position. As the world of work fluctuates, the demand for our services and the types of services required, are changing. At the Centre for Applied Positive Psychology (CAPP), the UK-based consultancy where I work, our motto is *the smallest thing to make the biggest difference.* It is a timely credo very much in line with what most leaders and companies are looking for.

What are strengths?

Although many philosophers, psychologists and consultants offer differing definitions of strengths, I am less concerned with issues of *who is right?* and more interested in *which models work best?* At CAPP we use a simple model to explain strengths. Strengths are pre-existing capacities in thought or behaviour that are both authentic and energising and lead to optimal performance when employed. In simpler terms, strengths are those tendencies that excite you, that seem to come naturally, and which make you shine. Two elements of this definition are useful. Firstly, it suggests (and I truly believe) that everyone has many strengths although they may not always be aware of them and/ or may not have developed them to full measure. Secondly, the fact that strengths are *energising* give us a handy diagnostic tool for noticing when and where we are employing our best traits. When I train groups on the strengths approach, I am often asked for the basic rationale for focusing on strengths. Common sense often tells us to do precisely the opposite: if our strengths come naturally to us, doesn't it make more sense to spend energy overcoming our weaknesses? As sensible as this question may be, neither research nor anecdotal evidence supports the weakness approach over the strengths approach. Studies of businesses by the Gallup Organization, for instance, show that top managers spend disproportionately more time with high performers as they try to match talents to tasks[1]. 1 Similarly, psychological research links the use of strengths to increased positivity and lower incidences of depression[2]. For this reason I call strengths the *back door to positivity.* There is a direct, causal connection between the kind of positivity and energy associated with strengths and better customer evaluations: less absenteeism, lower

---

1   Clifton, D & Harter, JK. 2003. "Investing in strengths". In K Cameron, J Dutton, & R Quinn, (Eds). *Positive Organizational Scholarship: Foundations of a New Discipline.* San Francisco, CA: Berrett-Koehler Publishers. pp 111–121.

2   Seligman, MEP, Steen, T, Park, N, & Peterson, C. 2005. "Positive psychology progress: Empirical validation of interventions". *American Psychologist*, 60:410–421.

staff turnover, and a higher rate of colleagues[3]. This is not to say that individuals should turn a blind eye to their weaknesses. Indeed, they should work to keep these from creating problems. But where actual development is concerned, there is more to be gained from cultivating strengths rather than weaknesses. I typically explain the relation between strengths and weaknesses using the metaphor of a sailboat. If there is a leak (a weakness) then it is vital to attend to it so that the boat (you or your organisation) does not sink. But simply fixing the leak will not actually get you anywhere – it is the sails (strengths) that propel the boat forward. Thus for very different reasons, attention to both strengths and weaknesses is important.

Strengths are especially relevant to coaches in the current global recession. Identifying and using strengths, both at the individual and the team level, is a way to get *more productivity for less.* Unleashing strengths improves performance without commensurate expenditure on training or education. In addition, a strengths focus can actually increase engagement and job satisfaction in these uncertain times. Strengths coaching is also relevant also because it is a useful approach for coaching people through outplacement. Finally, a strengths approach is well suited to leadership development. The current business climate mandates new styles of leadership. Strengths can be used both to develop flexible, effective leaders and to help these top executives and managers to identify their best personnel assets.

Four powerful strategies for using strengths in coaching

1. Although most seasoned coaches are familiar with the idea of helping clients take stock of their personal resources and best qualities, not everyone is sure of the best way to do this. Coaches usually work with an *identify and use* model of strengths development where they help a client to identify a strength and then brainstorm ways in which to use this resource. Although this is a commonsense approach, we at CAPP believe more can be done to develop and deploy strengths for

---

3   Lyubomirsky, S, King, L, & Diener, E. 2005. "The benefits of frequent positive affect: Does happiness lead to success?" *Psychological Bulletin*, 131:803–855.

maximum effectiveness. We believe, for example, that it is necessary first to build a large strength's vocabulary. The more a coach has a specific language for describing and understanding strengths, the more he or she is able to identify them in clients and facilitate their development. Practise this crucial first step by paying attention to the people around you: what are they excited about, what are they proud of, what are they looking forward to? Whenever you see these spikes of enthusiasm, you know you are narrowing in on a specific strength. It can be fun to try and create a name for it. For instance, I once had a client who would consistently put off his work until just before the deadline. This work style caused him no end of worry and guilt. The interesting aspect of his case was that his work was always completed on time (although at the last minute) and was always of a superior quality. What if it turned out that my client was not a *procrastinator* as he had labelled himself but an *incubator* – someone who subconsciously considers ideas and then is able to rise to the challenge and work well under pressure? As soon as I suggested this new label, my client felt relieved, motivated, and energised. He recognised that what he had was a gift and that what distinguished him from procrastinators was his consistent ability to produce superior work. The wonderful thing is that there is really no end to the strengths that we see in everyday life. Try identifying new strengths in your clients; have fun creating labels and specific definitions for them. The larger your strengths vocabulary, the better you will be able to in facilitating your client's strength development.

2. The second strengths-based coaching strategy is *identifying strengths,* a skill we at CAPP call *strengths spotting.* Although it makes sense, coaches sometimes do not know how to do this. There are a number of formal assessments available for identifying client's strengths (such as CAPP's own Realise2 measure, which will be previewed at our conference on April 1, or the free, but much more simplistic Values in Action assessment). These assessments, available online, typically ask respondents to answer a number of questions and then provide feedback about top strengths and weaknesses. In an interview or

coaching format, I often recommend using a *past–present–future* exercise, wherein you need ask only three questions:

- What is something you are proud of from the past?

- What energises you in the present?

- What are you looking forward to in the future.

As you listen to the answers to these questions, try to pay attention to when your client becomes particularly animated physically or verbally and then try to label the strength you are hearing or seeing. It is shocking how fruitful these apparently simple questions can be. At a training session I conducted in Toronto last month, for example, I asked a participant to *talk briefly about whatever it is you are looking forward to in the next month.* She spoke for only half a minute but the group was able to identify half a dozen strengths ranging from *creativity* (generating new ideas and presenting novel solutions to problems) to *catalyst* (someone who is the focal point for dynamic change). In cases where we did not have a ready label for a strength we simply made one up, or asked the participant to give it a name.

STRENGTHS

Optimal functioning
Development and Performance

Authentic   Energising

Pre-existing
capacity

- Behaving
- Thinking
- Feelling

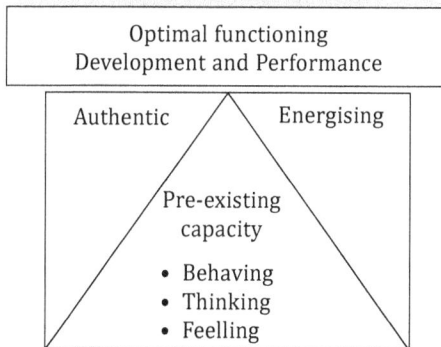

© Average to A+ by Alex Linley 2008

137

3. Once you have identified your client's strengths, it is time to get to the serious business of helping those strengths blossom. Many people mistakenly believe that because strengths come naturally, they require little or no active development. Nothing could be further from the truth. People frequently make the mistake of both *under*-and-*over* using their strengths. In the former case, people are either not aware of their strengths or do not have the situational opportunities to deploy them. As a coach, you are able to work with clients and help them to take ownership of their own best qualities and facilitate a better understanding of the situations most likely to bring out the best in them. In the case of over-using strengths, clients often misuse their abilities by not recognising when a situation is inappropriate or when a particular strength is producing diminishing returns. A person may rate highly in the strength of humour, for example, which is a terrific asset that can be helpful in stimulating creativity and resolving conflict. But there are certain situations such as those that require urgency or sanctity, where humour is not always appropriate. Learning to *turn the strength down* can be just as helpful to client effectiveness as learning to *turn it up*. Merely pointing out to clients that a strength can be over-used is often the first step to their using their strengths more effectively.

4. Finally, strengths themselves can be used to address weaknesses. While strengths often lead to our most obvious successes, they are also useful in compensating for those areas in which we perform poorly. Other solutions for managing weaknesses include designing situations in which weaknesses become largely irrelevant and collaborating with others who counterbalance your weaknesses. It is important for your clients to remember that they need not waste too much time and energy trying to develop weaknesses into strengths. It is far more efficient to spend that same investment of personal resources on managing weaknesses (stopping that leak) and developing strengths (raising those sails!).

For many of us, the economic woes we read about in the paper each day or face every morning when we arriving at the office may take a heavy psychological toll. Maintaining enthusiasm, positivity and a flourishing business can seem like a tall order under such circumstances. Fortunately, the strengths approach offers a low cost alternative to despair. Harnessing the best personnel assets already at hand is a great way to promote a more positive organisational culture, more individual and team productivity, and more employee engagement.

References

"For further reading please see Alex Linley's excellent *Average to A+: Realising strengths in yourself and others* (CAPP Press, 2008).

Clifton, D & Harter, JK. 2003. "Investing in strengths". In K Cameron, J Dutton, & R Quinn, (Eds). *Positive Organizational Scholarship: Foundations of a New Discipline*. San Francisco, CA: Berrett-Koehler Publishers. pp 111–121.

Seligman, MEP, Steen, T, Park, N, & Peterson, C. 2005. "Positive psychology progress: Empirical validation of interventions". *American Psychologist*, 60:410–421.

Lyubomirsky, S, King, L, & Diener, E. 2005. "The benefits of frequent positive affect: Does happiness lead to success?" *Psychological Bulletin*, 131:803–855.

❖ ❖ ❖ ❖

SECTION D

Managers as Coaches

- Creating a Coaching Culture Within an Organisation – an Organisational Case Study by **Dr Antoinette Gmeiner**

- Equipping Managers to Coach by **Penny Abbott** and **Peter Beck**

- Developing Leadership Talent: Turning Managers into Coaches by **Kathy Bennett** and **Helen Minty**

Creating a Coaching Culture Within an Organisation – An Organisational Case Study

Dr Antoinette Gmeiner

Coaching is the art of bringing out the greatness in people in a way that honours the integrity of the human spirit. It is both an innate human capacity and a teachable skill, which has now become a new way of working with people within a corporate context.

> **Dr Antoinette Gmeiner** is the CEO of Orion Business Solutions and director of OBS Coach House. She is a Master Executive Coach and has extensive coaching experience on EXCO and Board level. Dr Sandra Perkins, her business partner, is the joint CEO in Orion Business Solutions and OBS Coach House. They have been coaching for more than thirteen years and have established an internal Coaching Programme for the Orion Group, where fifteen teams are being coached on a monthly basis. Dr Gmeiner and Dr Perkins supervise the team coaching sessions, and also coach a few of the teams themselves.

Although the latest and hottest trend to invade the workplace, coaching is not new. It is a new derivative of the greatest thinking in self-improvement since the turn of the twentieth century.

Coaching found its place in history, and recently in the business world, when it exploded into the corporate environment in the 1990s. Today, workplace coaching includes dozens of speciality fields (just like medicine) for every kind of business concern, including personal career coaching, transition and merger coaching, start-up ventures and entrepreneurial coaching, executive leader coaching, team coaching, and what many call life coaching.

Coaching exists for every type and size of business – from small one-man operations to the huge top Fortune 500 companies. Coaching has proved a worthy investment during its short, but remarkable history.

Who uses coaching?

Coaching is used by hundreds of thousands of great business leaders who want to develop their people by believing in them, challenging them, supporting them, giving them more positive than negative feedback, and making sure they take care of themselves.

Traditionally, coaching has focused on goals and objectives defined within the veil of confidentiality of the coaching intervention. The coaching process has been viewed as an isolated intervention, and the value and impact of coaching was challenged time and again.

Today, in a new world of work, coaching has shifted from a single event to being part of a landscape, impacting business growth, customer service, profitability, and above-market sustainable growth.

A coaching intervention can no longer just be a conversation in isolation. To ensure the effectiveness of any coaching intervention in an organisation, it needs to be informed by the strategy of the organisation.

A case study: a coaching journey to create coaching culture

What follows is a case study on how an organisation embarked on a coaching journey to entrench a coaching culture within the organisation. The ultimate goal was to enhance engagement of employees and ensure productivity.

In 1996, the ORION Group, a property and hotel owning group, embarked on a Team Coaching Intervention. The CEO at the time shared his concerns with the coaches. He wanted to create a team-based organisation to enhance productivity and performance. He wanted to grow and build the organisation, and needed a programme of some sort to enable this to happen.

He expressed the following concerns at the time:

- Employees functioned in silos and shared very little information.

- There was lack of commitment and engagement as perceived by him.

- Absenteeism rates were high.

- There was high staff turnover.

- There were increased incidents of disciplinary action.

- There was no or little buy-in into the vision and strategy of the organisation.

The coaches, coming from a research background, decided to embark on focus group interviews to determine the experiences of employees working in the organisation.

A central question was asked namely:

"How do you experience working in this organisation currently?"

The second question asked, was:

"What recommendations do you have to establish a high-performance culture?"

The following themes emerged from the content analysis:

- Employees felt that decisions were made "top-down" and they were not involved in the decision-making process.

- Although they knew the CEO had a vision and a mission, they were unclear about the meaning thereof.

- Values were not supported by processes.

- Lack of trust resulted in lack of motivation, silo thinking, and lack of communication and problem solving.

- There was lack of self-awareness and awareness of strengths and weaknesses of other team members.

- There was a lack of clear role clarification.

The employees made the following recommendations for building a high-performance culture:

- Alignment to the core ideology of the organisation.

- Clear buy-in and understanding of the values of the organisation.

- Clear job profile and measures of performance – aligned to the strategy.

- Clear goals.

- Building trust.

- Autonomy to make own decisions and take responsibility.

- Regular feedback on performance.

- Building of self-awareness and interpersonal skills.

- A forum to have open and candid conversations.

- Fun and celebrations.

- Reward and recognition.

Based on these results, coaches embarked on a coaching journey 11 years ago. This was the beginning of entrenching a coaching culture within the organisation.

It all started by establishing a central coaching department, with a CEC (Chief Executive Coach) taking responsibility for the coaching programme.

The CEC decided to use internal as well as external coaches. Providing a fresh perspective from the outside, external coaches have the ability to look at the business from another perspective, often asking the "stupid" questions that can elicit the most meaning.

All coaches were selected carefully, based on certain selection criteria, one of which was accredited coaching training.

Supervision was an integral part of the coaching programme, and every coach who was part of the coaching programme had to attend monthly supervision sessions.

An organisation-specific coaching paradigm was designed, and was followed by all coaches to ensure alignment of the coaching intervention and to make sure all coaches were "on the same page" at all times.

The annual team coaching programme was informed by the company strategy and core ideology to ensure alignment to the ultimate goal – a high-performance culture. This was mandated by the EXCO team, together with input from all coaches.

The very important first step in entrenching the coaching culture in any organisation is obtaining buy-in from the top. In this organisation, all EXCO members were trained as coaches (accredited training through the University of Johannesburg).

This EXCO also participated in a team coaching intervention to support the coaching initiative as role models, and to live the vision of a "team-based" organisation.

Members of line management were also in team coaching, and received training as coaches and mentors. This empowered them to have "crucial coaching conversation" with the next level on a daily basis. (This is a shorter, three-day training intervention.)

Cascading of coaching from line management downwards to all other levels of the organisation was assessed on a monthly basis, with clear measurement indicators. The annual team coaching intervention and value on investment was measured on an annual basis. There is no clear ROI (Return on Investment) as a precise and specific financial calculation cannot be done accurately, because there are too many variables at play. The coaches used a measurement and a form of assessment, known as VOI (Value on Investment).

The VOI was done through a qualitative self-assessment and measurement, based on the programme for the year. Coachees were asked to rate themselves at the beginning of the year and then again at the end of the year, to ascertain changes in behaviour.

A 360-degree assessment was also done, where all team members' managers as well as EXCO were asked to rate their own team's performance in terms of behavioural shifts made during that year.

Clearly, the introduction of a coaching style of leadership involves more than simply training EXCO and managers in coaching skills and competencies. Developing a sustainable coaching culture appears to be a culture-change programme in its own right. Change begins to happen when a compelling business case for coaching is shared in the whole organisation, and when EXCO and managers experience the power of coaching themselves.

Today, eleven years later, the same principles are still in practice, and the evidence of success is in place. Employees describe their alignment as "engagement". They feel empowered in understanding the vision and mission of the organisation. They provide active input into strategy and they have accountability and responsibility in their daily encounters.

The journey has not been without challenges, but the coaching culture is close to being embedded, and all the processes and systems within the organisation are aligned to the team-based coaching philosophy. Our journey continues and we are excited to report on further research as we write up our results.

Confucius said:

"I hear and I forget, I see and I understand, I do and I remember."

❖ ❖ ❖ ❖

Equipping Managers to Coach

by Penny Abbott and Peter Beck

Coaching is increasingly recognised as an important tool in performance management within the global context. Many organisations are expecting line managers to coach employees, but managers often find coaching difficult. The good news is that with the correct training and support, line managers can excel at coaching. Penny Abbott and Peter Beck show us how managers can be prepared to fulfil this important role. They provide us with a practical coaching model that can be readily applied within organisations.

Penny and Peter are founding Partners and Directors of Clutterbuck Associates South Africa, a leading consultancy in the support of organisations' coaching and mentoring programmes.

Peter Beck runs his own consulting business specialising in change and diversity, and has recently added retirement living to his portfolio. He has a background as an HR practitioner with over 12 years' operational/line experience and 18 years' organisational development, with specific interest and experience in performance and change management, graduate and fast-track development, discrimination management and management, of diversity/relationship issues. He is currently active in the HIV/AIDS field in South Africa and has undertaken similar work in West and East Africa. He joined the University of Stellenbosch Business School as Faculty head for the FNB Management Development Programme in 2010. He is a Chartered HR Practitioner Generalist, a Mentor with the SA Board for People Practice, and an Advisory Board member for the International Standards for Mentoring Programmes in Employment (ISMPE). He is also a facilitator for Understanding Racism/Sexism/Classism and Developing Good Practice.

Penny Abbott uses her experience in management and leadership development, gained during her long and successful career in Human Resource Management, as the basis for her consultancy work in the field of coaching and mentoring. She has an MPhil from the University of Johannesburg in Human Resource Development and is engaged in doctoral research at the same institution. She is actively involved in Coaches and Mentors of South Africa and works in the Research & Definitions Committee, as well as leading the Mentoring Special Interest Group. She is a Master HR Practitioner and a Mentor with the SA Board for People Practice.

Clutterbuck Associates South Africa. *Coaching for Performance. Mentoring for Growth.* http://www.mentoring.co.za/.

A recent survey in the United Kingdom showed that over 70 percent of organisations use coaching within their organisations to facilitate growth and development. Of these organisations, 44 percent offer coaching to all employees, while about 40 percent offer coaching only to senior managers and executives. The latest ASTD report on the South African training industry shows a very slight increase in the use of mentoring and coaching by South African organisations, from 70 percent in 2007 to about 72 percent in 2008.

Who is doing the coaching?

According to a new book by Garvey, Stokes and Megginson, the CIPD 2007 survey showed that in the UK, "only a minority of organisations train their managers to coach, and only 7 percent completely agree that coaching is part of the line manager's job". However, it would appear that this is changing.

Previous CIPD research shows that coaching is increasingly seen as the responsibility of line management. Our 2008 *Learning and Development Survey* reports that 53 percent of respondents were increasingly asking line management to coach and mentor as part of their role, and only 5 percent were expecting them to do it less. By contrast, coaching by external practitioners had increased in only 38 percent of the sample and had decreased in around a fifth. It is quite clear, therefore, that there is a trend towards using line management as the main delivery mechanism for organisational coaching. This varies, however, from the use of some coaching behaviours or techniques to the deployment of line managers as internal coaches.

So far, there is no corresponding research in South Africa that indicates whether coaching is regarded as part of a line manager's role. It may be that the situation here is different, given the changes in demographics of line managers as a result of Employment Equity. This may mean that newer, less experienced, managers are not expected to coach their subordinates, and that this role is rather allocated to technical experts or external coaches.

What are line managers supposed to coach?

The role most often attributed to coaching by line managers is that of training an employee newly allocated to a specific task and also of coaching for improvement where performance has not been satisfactory. Coaching often begins with the coachee unable to perform a task, for example, creating and delivering a presentation. The coach initially needs to help the learner to achieve a transition from inability to basic ability (from *I can't do it* to *I can*); then from basic ability to competence (*I can do it well*). This is often called "skills coaching". Performance coaches may work on the second half of this sequence, or may work with problems that a coachee has encountered, in trying to achieve competence. One example of differentiation between types of coaching is used in the Interaction Management training modules of DDI, which distinguish between Coaching for Success (which occurs prior to the employee's embarking on a new project or task) and Coaching for Improvement (which reflects on what happened as a project or task was completed). Both types of coaching are firmly allocated to line management. Subject matter experts usually perform technical skills coaching, and this is often included in learnership programmes.

In order to achieve the highest levels of performance, employees need to achieve the highest level of competence. In SAQA terms, it is that of "reflexive competence", defined as "the ability to integrate performance with understanding so as to show that the learner is able to adapt to changed circumstances appropriately and responsibly and to explain the reason behind an action". This definition has many similarities with the requirements described by Garvey *et al.* for a knowledge worker in modern organisations. They note that such knowledge workers need abilities such as "time management, relationships, communication skills creativity, emotions, metacognitive skills, and a capacity to reflect upon behaviour and experience". If these abilities are all required from employees, it can be argued that it is the line manager's responsibility to help employees to acquire these abilities.

Many line managers would probably not rate themselves highly on their ability to coach on such requirements. A case study on internal coaching at the BBC describes how the organisation trained up internal coaches over a period of time and how some of these coaches moved from their line responsibilities to become full-time internal coaches. Such an arrangement can provide a good combination of the advantages of an internal coach (knowledge of the organisation, internal networks, etcetera) and the advantages of in-depth training that normally come with an external coach.

How should internal coaches be trained?

One of the major constraints in training managers to be coaches is their time, so to require them to attend coaching training can be difficult. In an international project managed by one of the authors in a very large multi-national company, such training was incorporated into training in performance management processes, which was made compulsory for all managers at all levels. The training consisted of a two-day programme, and review sessions were built in for the months to come. When planning coach training for managers, companies often request that the training be as short as possible. While some awareness of the issues involved in coaching can be achieved in a few hours, proper coaching skills cannot be acquired in any training process that does not involve extensive skills practice in the training sessions, practice on the job, and review sessions thereafter.

We recommended that companies build a structure within which managers (and technical experts) can acquire additional coaching skills and thereby additional status as a developmental resource within the company. Higher levels of this structure could then allow for training in advanced coaching skills, thereby enabling the coach to address some of the more general learning and development needs. Many experienced experts and managers welcome the opportunity to gain such skills, and this can be a valuable retention tool for such people.

A practical coaching model for line managers

The line manager as coach needs to apply a systematic approach to helping people achieve personal change. Informal discussions on the job are not sufficient to achieve real change. Models such as the GROW model are helpful in structuring a specific coaching conversation, but the coaching role is much wider than that. This seven-step coaching model is simple to explain and easy to use. The framework below sets out the seven key steps to follow:

Step 1: Identify the need to improve

- Where do the development priorities lie for the coachee?

- Where will a performance improvement have the biggest business impact?

- **Step 2: Observe and gather evidence**

- Identify sources of evidence that will help coachees understand the reality of their situation.

- Wherever possible, cross-check one source against another to make sure that the findings are accurate.

- Determine the current level of coachee performance as a baseline against which to measure their progress.

Step 3: Motivate to set and own personal improvement targets

- Help coachees to understand that they have a development need and that they can improve.

- Help the coachee to agree to a **S**pecific, **M**easurable, **A**chievable, **R**elevant and **T**ime-based (SMART) target.

- Define and clarify what you are both trying to achieve.

Step 4: Help to plan how to achieve those targets

- Ensure that the target is broken into small enough steps to be able to track progress.

- Listen to the coachee's ideas about development opportunities.

- Identify potential development opportunities for the coachee.

- Guide coachees, helping them choose the opportunities which are right for their needs.

Step 5: Create opportunities to practise the desired skills

- Talk with coachees to identify the most effective development activities, targeted precisely at their individual needs.

- Create opportunities to develop or practise the target skills (for example, work-based projects).

Step 6: Observe in action and give objective feedback

- Review the coachees performance.

- The emphasis is on the coachees' giving their assessment of their own performance first. This allows the coachees to reflect on what they've learnt through the process before the coach gives feedback.

Step 7: Support and help to work through setbacks

• Identify further options to accelerate or reinforce learning.

The seven steps often form a continuous cycle. It is quite common for a coach and coachee to be at step 1 on one issue and step 7 on another. What matters is that you go through all the steps for every coaching issue. Should you leave any out, there is a real danger that the coaching effort will not show the desired results.

Can all line managers be trained to coach effectively?

Managers often find it difficult to coach. This could be because of a lack of time in addition to other pressures. It could also be because they have adopted an inappropriate leadership style, whereby they avoid delegation and use a "tell-and-show" approach. While managers usually accept the need to coach, they often feel that they lack appropriate skills and tools. Careful and thorough training is therefore essential to build their confidence. The adoption of an appropriate coaching model is also important. Companies can run regular skills-building and support sessions as part of the programme to build a coaching culture within the organisation, ensuring that, "people at all levels are engaged in coaching, both formal and informal".

References

CIPD *Learning and Development Survey* 2008. The terms mentoring and coaching are used linked together in this survey so that coaching is not separated out.

Garvey, B, Stokes, P, & Megginson, D. 2007. *Coaching and Mentoring – Theory and Practice.* Sage Publications. p 128.

CIPD *Fact Sheet on Coaching.* http://www.cipd.co.uk/subjects/lrnanddev/coachmntor/coaching.htm?IsSrchRes=1 *Licence to Coach,* Coaching at Work, 4(2):24–27.

Clutterbuck, D & Megginson, D. 2005. *Making Coaching Work – creating a coaching culture.* CIPD.

❖ ❖ ❖ ❖

Developing Leadership Talent: Turning Managers into Coaches

by Kathy Bennett and Helen Minty

Increased communication with more sharing and openness; the identification of personal areas for future development; skills improvement and increased motivation. These are some of the spin-offs that one can expect organisationally when coaching managers to be coaches, not to mention the increased productivity which naturally results from good management/worker relations. Helen Minty and Kathy Bennett take us through their case study which brings these and many other dynamics into clear focus.

"When managers communicate a genuine interest in helping rather than evaluating their employees, they create opportunities for everyone to learn." (J Hunt and J Weintraub. 2002. *The Coaching Manager: Developing Top Talent in Business*.)

It was with this sentiment in mind that the following case study was begun. The client had a need for a long-term coaching intervention that would equip his managers to become effective coaches, entrench coaching as a leadership style and manage staff within his team as unique individuals. There is widespread agreement that coaching is an important facet of leadership, a powerful tool for improving performance, and an important process in talent management. And yet, coaching is not always carried out in a way that adds significant value, to the organisation, to those being coached, or those carrying out the coaching.

Intervention framework

The intervention was tackled over a year, dovetailing with the organisation's performance management system (see Figure 1). Each of the four phases was begun with a workshop to provide theoretical input and, more importantly, extensive skills practice. After each phase, managers tackled an assignment designed to transfer learning and skills into the work environment. While coaching in itself is not a difficult skill to learn, it is often tricky in application because each and every coaching situation or session is unique. Coaching is very much a skill learned on the job rather than in a classroom, and for this reason we opted to *coach the coaches* and provide ongoing supervision throughout the duration of the intervention. In this way, we supported and reinforced the managers' developing skills. Initially we met the managers each month for a two-hourly coaching session. After eight months, we reduced our meetings to once every second month to prepare them to take on full responsibility for coaching by the end of the intervention. To emphasise the importance of the intervention, performance as an effective coach was formally measured at the end of the intervention and was tied to a Key Performance Indicator which influenced each manager's performance bonus.

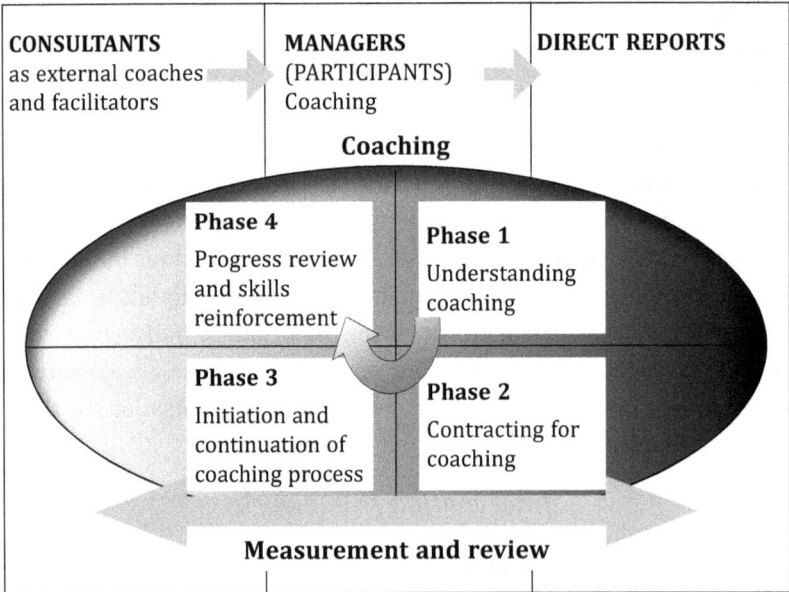

Figure 1: Intervention framework

Phase 1: Understanding coaching

We initiated the intervention with a workshop to introduce the concept of coaching and to make a convincing business case for it. Managers usually feel it takes up too much time they lack the necessary skills, and the organisation does not provide the structure for them to be effective as coaches. This workshop was aimed at challenging these assumptions and creating a meaningful context for coaching. As a first assignment following the workshop, each manager considered each of his or her members of staff.

We began our coaching of each manager with a discussion of the perceived strengths and development areas of each of their staff members, their career aspirations, and possible areas for coaching. The coaching of managers' direct reports focused not only on improving performance, but also on utilising employee strengths and offering new challenges (as a motivational and talent management strategy) to competent performers, as a motivational and talent management strategy.

Phase 2: Contracting for coaching

We believe that effective coaching hinges on a contract for coaching i.e. a unique, individual agreement between the employee and his manager. Our second phase commenced with a workshop to provide guidance regarding the process of designing this contract. After this workshop (in preparation for establishing specific coaching contracts for the following year with each person), managers reviewed staff development plans. During our coaching of the managers, we reviewed their preparation for these discussions and offered further guidance.

Phase 3: Initiation and continuation

Our third workshop kick-started the ongoing process of staff coaching. Managers learned core coaching skills, for both formal and ad hoc coaching. They had extensive practice through case studies and role plays. We introduced the concept of action learning and the setting of

159

specific assignments following each coaching session. We also provided the managers with a set of *coaching tools* in the form of written materials they could use to assist them in planning and running coaching sessions. These focused on a variety of different issues and offered suggestions for meaningful practice assignments which managers could set for their employees. They were also designed to help stimulate self-reflection and awareness in the person being coached. The post-workshop assignment required managers to prepare a coaching plan for their first coaching session with each of their staff members. The parallel coaching process initially involved a review of these coaching plans. It then continued with monthly coaching sessions of approximately two hours. Through the coaching logs of the process, we jointly reviewed the plans and actual outcomes for each past coaching session. We discussed what had actually happened in those sessions, what the plans were for future sessions, the assignments they had set, and how these had been completed by their staff members. We jointly reflected on what had gone well, what had not gone so well, and what each manager might do differently in future in order to be a more effective coach.

Phase 4: Review and reinforcement

We felt that sharing each manager's learning with the rest of the team was important. Not only did this offer additional opportunities for managers to learn from each other; it assisted in creating a shared team language and culture. In addition, it offers an opportunity to practice presentation skills. Taking confidentiality into account, the final phase workshop involved each manager presenting her personal coaching experiences. Some of the questions the managers answered are featured below, with some of the key points that they raised.

The most successful or rewarding experience as coaches:

- Breakthroughs in challenging coaching situations

- Significant shifts in competence, attitude or self insight

- Individuals who embraced the process, for example, took it into their personal life and

- Mentoring high potential individuals.

The most challenging or frustrating experience as coaches:

- Individuals not taking ownership for self-improvement

- Individuals lacking self-insight

- Dealing with less-open individuals, and

- Individuals making progress and then regressing.

The most significant personal learning:

- A better understanding of their direct reports and their needs

- The benefits of their own self-reflection

- Improved listening skills, and

- Improved patience and perseverance.

The most important benefits of coaching for their staff:

- Individuals taking responsibility for their own futures

- Increasing staff self awareness and self-confidence

- Increased staff participation

- Improved *big picture* understanding by staff, and

- Staff embracing the concept and process of coaching, for example, by the use of coaching *jargon* within the whole team.

One of our objectives was to create managers competent enough to coach effectively (see Figure 2 and Table 1). We therefore chose a benchmark coaching profile provided by *Kinlaw's Coaching Skills Inventory – CSI.*

Kinlaw asserts that a competent coach achieves an overall score of 3.98 out of a possible 5.00 when assessed using his questionnaire. All staff members who had been coached by their managers throughout the intervention completed Kinlaw's CSI questionnaire. The managers' average scores (a reflection of their staff members' perspective of their coaching competence) were then compared with the benchmark score of 3.98. Only one of the nine managers who took part in the intervention scored slightly below the benchmark, as can be seen in the results illustrated in Figure 2 below. CSI scores were linked with an individual Key Performance Indicator that formed part of the organisation's Performance Management process and influenced each manager's performance bonus.

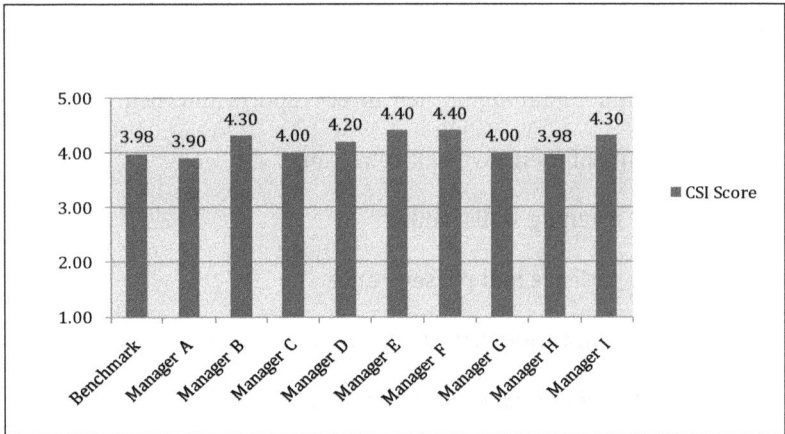

Figure 2: Managers' Coaching Competence Compared with Benchmark Coaching Profile

The other objective was to entrench coaching as an integral part of the leadership style within the team. We also asked each manager's staff to assess him using a customised questionnaire, designed to measure their perception of the value of the coaching process. Staff members were asked to respond to each of nine statements in terms of the extent to which they agreed with the statement. We received a total of 48 responses (see Table 1). Scores were pooled and an overall average was calculated.

We determined our target score as 3.5 – this being an average score for the overall management team. This reflected a perception midway between *agree* (3) and *agree strongly* (4). The management team achieved a score of 3.46, thereby meeting the target. We believed the overwhelmingly positive responses indicated that coaching had indeed become entrenched within the team. The only area where there was some disagreement was around career discussions. Through a focus-group process, this was investigated further, and we found that these concerns related to clarification of company policies.

Case study review

The client agreed that the intervention had indeed developed his managers' leadership skills and had entrenched coaching as a culture within his team. He said he had noted significant personal growth in each of his managers and that they had developed more effective relationships with their staff. He had also observed noticeable personal development and increased effectiveness in many of his managers' staff.

The managers taking part not only recognised improvements in their own coaching skills, but also acknowledged shifts in their thinking around the process of development itself. They commented as follows:

- They no longer looked at training as the only development option, but were employing a range of alternative strategies, tailored to individual needs.

- Most of their direct reports were performing more effectively, as a direct result of the coaching process.

- Coaching had taken their relationships with their people to a different level, that is, deeper and more open.

- Following significant breakthroughs, some of their most difficult coaching challenges finally became the most rewarding.

Managers' staff reported that the coaching process had added value to their growth and development, as well as to their work performance,

163

Table 1. Evaluation of managers' coaching by their staff members.

	Statements about the managers' coaching	Responses expressed as percentages (%)			
		1 Disagree strongly	2 Disagree	3 Agree	4 Agree strongly
1	Overall, I have personally benefited from the coaching carried out by my manager.	0	0	67	33
2	My relationship with my manager has benefited through regular coaching.	0	0	54	46
3	I have noticed positive changes in my manager's leadership style as a result of the coaching he or she has done with me.	0	8	63	29
4	The coaching assignments set by my manager have helped me to understand myself better.	0	0	37	63
5	The coaching assignments set by my manager have helped me to apply new knowledge and skills practically.	0	4	50	46
6	My job performance has improved as a direct result of coaching.	0	4	50	46
7	I have grown personally as a direct result of coaching.	0	4	50	46
8	The coaching process has encouraged me to take more responsibility for my personal and career development.	0	8	34	58
9	Since the coaching began, my manager has been facilitating more meaningful development and career planning discussions with me.	0	21	46	33

where they felt more engaged with their work and their team. Most direct reports said that the relationship with their manager had been enhanced through the intervention. Some specific comments included: "Coaching has increased communication, with more sharing and openness with my manager"; "Coaching has helped me to identify my development areas"; "There has been a definite skill improvement"; and "Coaching is motivational".

Critical success factors

There are a number of critical success and *learning for others* factors pertaining to the intervention that we would like to share with organisations which are considering developing their managers as coaches. These are as follows:

- The active support of senior management is essential for success

- The importance of coaching must compare with other results – for example, measurement of coaching skill competence linked with the organisation's performance management system

- The coaching process must be structured. Managers must hold formal coaching sessions, using a structured format, for example, GROW (Goal, Reality, Options, Wrap Up) with their direct reports, preferably on at least a monthly basis. In addition there should be ad hoc coaching, and the process should be documented, even if only briefly. There needs to be a brief formal process for planning and recording coaching sessions

- Managers and external coaches need to meet for parallel coaching sessions, that is, *coaching the coaches* on a regular basis. As stated above, coaching is a skill actually learned on the job. The support and reinforcement of a competent supervisor is vitally important for maximising the potential of an intervention to develop coaching competence

- The long-term nature of the process, versus a one-off skills training programme, should be recognised and implemented. This should include the format of workshops, assignments, and skills practices repeated throughout the year, and

- The importance of sharing the learning must be understood. This will reinforce the significance of learning from each other and assist in instilling coaching as a leadership culture.

❖ ❖ ❖ ❖

SECTION E

Coaching Models

- Working with Coaching Models by **Dr Sunny Stout Rostron**

- Working with Coaching Models: The Nested-Levels Model by **Dr Sunny Stout Rostron**

- Working with Coaching Models: The U-Process by **Dr Sunny Stout Rostron**

- How Can I Approach The Human Spirit? – The New Coach's Transformation **by David B Drake (Editor), Diane Brennan** and **Kim Gørtz**

- Sample of a Generic Mentorship/Coaching Agreement

Working with Coaching Models

by Dr Sunny Stout Rostron

This series of articles by Dr Sunny Stout Rostron introduces a variety of coaching models and gives examples of how to facilitate a coaching conversation using each one. In this first article, she focuses on the Purpose, Perspectives, Process Model and outlines how this model can be used to develop a structured approach to your coaching conversation, how to contract with the client, structure the entire coaching journey and guide your coaching conversation.

> **Sunny Stout Rostron**, DProf, MA, is an executive coach and consultant with a wide range of experience in leadership and management development, business strategy, and executive coaching. The author of seven books, including *Business Coaching Wisdom and Practice and Unlocking the Secrets of Business Coaching*, Sunny is a founding director of the Manthano Institute of Learning (Pty) Ltd and a director with Resolve Encounter Consulting.

Coaching models help us to understand the coaching intervention from a systems perspective, and to understand the need for "structure" in the interaction between coach and client. They offer flexibility and a structure for both the coaching conversation and the overall coaching journey.

Although models create a system within which coach and client work, it is essential that models are not experienced as either prescriptive or rigid. The coaching conversation is about the client, not the coach. If the model is too prescriptive, it means it is fulfilling the coach's agenda, rather than attempting to understand the client's issues.

What is a coaching model?

A *model* represents a system with an implied process. It is a metaphor or analogy used to help visualise and describe the journey. Models systemically visualise or represent a process that cannot be directly observed. In other words, a model represents more than you see. If you can develop a model that encompasses the coaching conversation and the entire coaching intervention, you will begin to work with considerably greater ease within your practice. A coaching model is representative of what happens, or will happen, in the coaching conversation (micro) and in the overall coaching intervention or journey (macro). I recommend working with simple models that represent both the micro- and macro-coaching interventions.

If you imagine that the model is the process you use to work with your client, it embodies all of your tools and techniques, including your question frameworks. So a model is a simple representation of the journey that can encompass the skills, experience and expertise that both the coach and client bring to the coaching conversation.

Which models to use?

The main purpose of this series is to introduce you to a variety of models, with examples of how to facilitate a coaching conversation using each one. The key principle I want to convey is that it is essential to adopt a structured approach to your coaching conversation. This does not mean that you cannot let the conversation grow and be explorative, but I am talking about structure as it relates to the bigger picture. That is the beauty of any model: having the freedom to explore within each part of the model.

The Purpose, Perspectives, Process model (see Figure 1) was developed by David Lane of the Professional Development Foundation (PDF) and the Work-Based Learning Unit at London's Middlesex University (Lane and Corrie, 2006).

Figure 1: Purpose, Perspectives, Process Model
Source: Lane and Corrie (2006)

- **Purpose (Where are we going and why?)**

What is your purpose in working with the client? Where are you going with this client? What does the client want to achieve? Where do they want to go in their overall journey with you as their coach?

For example, one client working in the telecoms industry said in our first session together: "I need your help because everybody in the organisation distrusts me and I'm in a pretty senior position. What can I do about it? I'm highly respected by those subordinate to me in position and disliked and mistrusted by those superior or equal to me in position." As coach, your questions will relate to client purpose, namely, "Where are we going and what's the reason for going there?" It is usually better to ask a "what" question rather than a "why" question. For example, "Why are we going there?" sounds intrusive and can create a defensive posture on the part of the client. "What" questions help to create a bigger picture of the journey; "what" creates perspective. This client's purpose was to "build alliances and trust with peers, colleagues and superiors throughout the organisation".

- **Perspectives (What will inform our journey?)**

What perspectives inform the journey for both coach and client? What informs our journey, that is, what informs the client and what informs the coach? Both coach and client come in with their individual backgrounds, experience, expertise, culture, values, motivations and assumptions that drive behaviour.

I recently had a call from a potential client within the energy industry. He was a general manager. We chatted about his perspective on his background, career and current job. We discussed his perspective in terms of his position within the organisation, his style of leading and managing his team of people, and the impact and influence of his age on his career prospects, and finally he said: "I have got as far as I can get with what I know now – and I need to know more, somehow".

We then discussed my perspective, namely, what informs the way I work with clients, and what informs my experience and expertise. Based on our mutual perspectives, he asked: "Would we have some kind of synchronicity or a match in order to work together?" He wanted to understand what models, tools and techniques I used as he wanted to create his own leadership development toolbox for his senior managers. He also wanted to understand how to handle mistakes: did I make them, and what would my education, training and work experience bring to our conversation? In this first contracting conversation, we worked through the model beginning with perspectives:

Perspectives: How we might bring our two worlds together

Purpose: What he ultimately wanted from the coaching experience, and

Process: How we would work together to achieve his outcomes.

- **Process (How will we get there?)**

Using this model helped me to begin to understand the above client's needs, to develop rapport and to identify not just his overall outcomes but a way to begin working together. At this stage of the model we contracted, set boundaries, agreed confidentiality matters, and outlined the fee-paying process and the development of a leadership development plan. We also agreed on timing (how often we would see each other and the individual client's line manager); what assessments would be useful for the individual client to complete; and how we would debrief those profiles. We discussed potential coaching assignments and timing for the overall contract (including termination and exit possibilities if either party was unhappy) and explored how to obtain line manager approval. Finally, we set up a separate meeting to agree on the process with the line manager and the group HR director.

How can this model help you?

This model can help you in three ways: to contract with the client; to structure the entire coaching journey; and to guide your coaching conversation. Out of this specific conversation emerged the client's purpose; the way our perspectives would fit together to help him to achieve his purpose; and the process within which we would work to achieve the outcomes desired.

This model can be used for the regular coaching conversations you have with your client. The client brings to the conversation a possible "menu" of topics to be discussed, or even just one particular topic. One of my clients in the media field came to me one day saying: "My purpose today is to understand why I am sabotaging my best efforts to delegate to my senior managers" (*purpose*). As the coach, I wanted to understand all of the perspectives underlying the client's aim for this conversation (*perspectives*), as well as to identify the various tools or techniques that could be used in the *process*.

The coaching conversation and the coaching journey

This model can represent the process for just one coaching conversation, but it can also represent the overall journey. For example, the client comes in with their **purpose**: "I would like to work with you; no one else will work with me as they find me too difficult". This client's purpose became to find a coach who would work with her, to help her to identify how she could not just develop the interpersonal skills to work successfully with others, but also demonstrate her new learning through visible behaviour change at work.

The coach and the client's **perspectives** will be unique and different. In working with the client, you bring not just perspective, but your observations as to how this client seems to be working within the organisational system.

In terms of **process**, the coach may ask the client to do a range of assessment profiles or you may shadow the client at work to experience how he or she facilitates meetings and interacts with customers, subordinates, superiors and colleagues.

Conclusion

Coach practitioners have a great deal of flexibility when working with coaching models. In my next article we will explore the use of the nested-levels model developed by New Ventures West (Weiss, 2004). I hope I have stimulated your appetite to further investigate coaching models.

References

Kolb, D. 1984. *Experiential learning: Experience as the source of learning and development.* Upper Saddle River, NJ: Prentice Hall.

Lane, DA & Corrie, S. 2006. *The modern scientist-practitioner: A guide to practice in psychology.* Hove: Routledge.

Stout Rostron, S. 2006. Interventions in the coaching conversation: Thinking, feeling and behaviour. Unpublished DProf dissertation. London: Middlesex University.

Note:

This article is adapted from *Business Coaching Wisdom and Practice: Unlocking the Secrets of Business Coaching* (2009, Johannesburg: Knowledge Resources) and was originally printed in The WABC e-zine: *Business Coaching Worldwide,* February 2009, Volume 5, Issue 1.

❖ ❖ ❖ ❖

Working with Coaching Models: The Nested-Levels Model

by Dr Sunny Stout Rostron

Coaching expert Dr Sunny Stout Rostron says that it is important to consider different coaching models in order to become more effective in our coaching. Here she explores the nested-levels model of coaching, which first looks at the horizontal level of "doing", then goes a level deeper to "learning", and finally it reaches a third "ontological" level, where new knowledge emerges about oneself and the world.

Coaching as an experiential learning conversation[1]

One of the core areas where coaches work with clients is in the area of learning. However, the conversation with your client centres on what is meaningful to them. If significance and relevance are to emerge from the coaching conversation, it does not matter what is relevant to you; it matters what is relevant to them. It is therefore important to be aware of your own assumptions about what the client needs.

If you are guiding, directing, and giving your clients all the information they need, it will be difficult for them to ever be free of you. It is better if the client embodies new learning personally and physiologically, as you cannot do their learning for them. What you do as a coach is to help them reconstruct their own thinking and feeling to gain perspective and become self-directed learners. At the end of each coaching session with my clients, we integrate their learning with the goals they have set, confirming to what action, if any, they are committed:

- **Vision:** Refine their vision – Where is the client going?

- **Strategy:** Outline the strategy – How is the client going to achieve their vision?

---

1   "Learning conversations" refers to research into learning conversations and self-organised learning, developed by S Harri-Augstein and LF Thomas (1991:24).

- **Outcomes:** What are the specific outcomes that need to be accomplished in the next few weeks in order to work toward achieving the vision and putting the strategy into action?

- **Learning:** Help the client to summarise what has been gained from the session in order to underline self-reflection. Assist the client in understanding that he or she is responsible for his or her own thinking, doing and being.

Nested-levels model

Although models create a system within which coach and client *learn*, it is essential that models are not experienced as either prescriptive or rigid. If the model is inflexible, it means it is fulfilling the coach's agenda, rather than attempting to understand the client's issues.

This nested-levels model was developed by New Ventures West (Weiss, 2004), and introduces the concept of horizontal and vertical levels in coaching models. The nested-levels model works first at the horizontal level of "doing" eventually moves into deeper "learning" one level down; and reflects about self, others and experience at a third "ontological" level, where new knowledge emerges about oneself and the world (see Figure 1).

In her article, Pam Weiss talks about the two different camps of coaches. In jest, I call them the Jo'burg versus the Cape Town camp. The Jo'burg camp says: "I'm the expert, let me fix you", while the Cape Town camp says, "You are perfect and whole and have all of your own answers". Joking aside, each of these camps comes up short, even though coaches often fall into one or the other. The role of coaching is actually about developing human beings. It is not really about, "I have the expertise" versus "you already have all your own answers".

The expert approach

Contrary to what experts may think, clients are not broken and are not in need of fixing. Clients may be anxious, stressed, nervous, overworked

What	DOING	
How	LEARNING	
Who	WAY OF BEING	

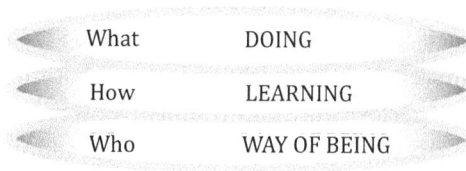

Figure 1: Nested-levels model
Source: Adapted from Weiss (2004)

and even narcissistic – but they don't need fixing. They are mostly healthy human beings going about their jobs and lives, experiencing their own human difficulties. Your job as coach is to help the clients learn for themselves, so that when you are no longer walking alongside them, they have become "self-directed" learners (Harri-Augstein & Thomas, 1991) and do not need you any more. The second view on "expertise" also has limitations. The role of expertise is that, as coach, you are an expert; but coaching is not about the coach giving all the answers; that tends to be the role of the consultant, namely, to find solutions for the client.

The "you-have-all-the-answers" approach

The "you have all the answers" assumption is partially true, but there are several limitations. The first is that we all have blind spots and it is your job as coach to help the client to identify his or her blind spots. Secondly, it is perhaps a bit of "mythical" thinking that the client has all of the answers already; the flip side of that argument is that, if it does not work out, the client assumes blame and fault. In other words: "If I have all the answers, I should be able to do it myself without help". If that is not the case, they could feel: "Oh dear, if I am not able to do it myself, then perhaps I'm a failure."

Both of these approaches are "horizontal", that is, they skim the surface of the work you can do with the client. Both help people to maintain the lives they currently have. The expert "Jo'burg" approach helps the client to do it better, faster, and more efficiently; and the "Cape Town" approach may withhold key insights and observations from the coach that could help to build the client's awareness of his or her blind spots. What is important, rather than "fixing" the client, is the skill of "observation" on the part of the coach. There is no problem in helping the client to do it better, faster or more efficiently – that is often what the organisation hopes for in terms of performance improvement. However, it is important for the client to gain the learning he or she needs to address blind spots and to build his or her own internal capacity and competence.

Learning level

If you continue to help people to accomplish tasks, achieve goals and keep on "doing", they risk falling into the trap of being "busy" and possibly overwhelmed. They may not, however, necessarily get the "learning" they need in order to develop self-awareness and self-management. I know this trap of being excessively busy all too well. If we keep doing without reflection, we eventually burn out. To keep individual executives performing better and better, they need to work at one level lower – at the level of learning. They need to learn how to "do the doing" better. As soon as executives begin to work with a coach, they begin the possibility of working at one or two levels deeper.

As coach, you will be asking questions to help clients reflect, review, and gain useable knowledge from their experience. In the nested-levels model, the higher levels don't include the lower ones, but the lower levels include the higher ones. We need to help clients to address their purpose one level down, at the level of learning. At this level you may ask questions such as: "How are you doing? What are you doing? What are you feeling? How are your peers/colleagues experiencing you/this? What is and what isn't working? What is useful learning for you here? What needs to change, and how?"

The level of being and becoming

The third and fourth levels of the coaching intervention using this model are those of **who the client is** and **who the client wishes to become** in terms of thinking, feeling and being (these are sometime referred to as the ontological levels).

Your questions move from "What do they need to do?" and "How do they need to do it?" (*doing*) to:

- How does their style of learning impact on how they do what they do?

- What do they need to learn in order to improve their thinking, behaviour, feelings, performance or leadership? (*learning*)

- What do they need to understand and acknowledge about themselves?

- Who are they?

- How do they be who they are?

- What needs to change? (*being and becoming*)

So what assists people in getting things done? Above all, it is about clarifying goals, creating action steps, taking responsibility, and being accountable. In order to perform more effectively, we need to help clients shift down a gear to learn how to work with competence (a set of skills) rather than just learning a specific new skill.

Learning

Your job as coach is to help the clients open themselves up to the possibility of learning something new, and to help them relate to themselves and others at a deeper level. When using the nested-levels model, you could ask questions such as:

1. What is it that your client(s) want to **do**? What is their aim or purpose in working with you?

2. What do they need to **learn** in order to make the change? What in their thinking, feeling and behaviour needs to change in order to do the doing better? How can they use their own experience to learn what is needed?

3. How do, and how will, their thoughts, feelings and behaviour impact on how they "**be** who they are" and "who is it that they

want to **become**"? In this way, we work at horizontal and vertical levels. At the end of the day, the client's new attitudes, behaviours, motivations and assumptions begin to impact positively on his or her own performance and relationships with others.

Our aim with this model is to shift any limiting sense of who the client is so that they can interact and engage with the world in new ways. As clients begin to shift, it has an impact on others with whom they interact in the workplace. It also means addressing issues systemically, from a holistic perspective, whether those issues revolve around health, stress, anxiety, performance, or relationships with others. Our task as coaches is to widen the circle, enlarge the perspective of the clients and help him or her to learn from their own experience how to reach their potential.

A great way to start any coaching intervention is to ask your clients to tell their life story. The coach begins to understand some of the current issues and presenting challenges, and begins to observe patterns of thinking, feeling and behaviour. Because we work with Kolb's theory of "understanding experience in order to transform it into useable knowledge", this model helps us to determine the context in which the client operates, where individual and systemic problems may be occurring and organisational values and culture impact on individuals and teams. It is at this level that the coach's ability to observe, challenge and ask appropriate questions can be most transformational.

Conclusion

Coaching models like this help us to understand the coaching intervention from a systems perspective, analysing the "structure" of the interaction between coach and client. They offer great insights in terms of how we can become more effective coaches.

References

Kolb, D. 1984. *Experiential Learning: Experience as the Source of Learning and Development.* Upper Saddle River, NJ: Prentice Hall.

Stout Rostron, S. 2006. *Interventions in the Coaching Conversation: Thinking, Feeling and Behaviour.* Unpublished DProf dissertation. London: Middlesex University.

Weiss, P. 2004. *"The Three Levels of Coaching".* Available at: *http://www. newventureswest.com/three_levels.pdf.*

Stout Rostron, S. 2009. *Business Coaching Wisdom and Practice: Unlocking the Secrets of Business Coaching.* Johannesburg: Knowledge Resources.

Note: This article is adapted from *Business Coaching Wisdom and Practice: Unlocking the Secrets of Business Coaching* (2009, Johannesburg: Knowledge Resources) and was originally printed in The WABC e-zine: *Business Coaching Worldwide,* February 2009, Volume 5, Issue 1.

❖ ❖ ❖ ❖

Working with Coaching Models: The U-Process

by Dr Sunny Stout Rostron

In this article, Dr Sunny Stout Rostron continues to investigate coaching models that influence the work of business and executive coaches worldwide. Here she examines the use of the U-process model for coaching individuals and groups.

Coaching as an experiential learning conversation: The U-process

The U-process is sometimes known as the process of transition. In the field of coaching, this U-process is typically represented in Scharmer's model of change. In the process of transition, the client can move from anxiety, through happiness, fear, threat, guilt, denial, disillusionment, depression, gradual acceptance, and hostility, to moving forward.

The U-process is considered a mid-range change theory with a sense of an emerging future. Scharmer's process moves the client through different levels of perception and change, with differing levels of action which follow. The three main elements are *sensing*, *presencing* and *realising*. These represent the three basic aspects of the U (Figure 1).

This process helps the client to work at different levels of perception and change, and allows different levels of actions to follow. All three are extensions of the learning process. As the coach and client move into the U, **sensing** is about observing and becoming one with the world; **presencing,** moving to the bottom of the U, is about retreating and reflecting and allowing an inner knowing to emerge; and **realising,** as you move out of the "U", is about acting swiftly and with a natural flow from the knowledge and understanding that has emerged.

Sensing
Observe, observe, observe
Become one with the world

Realising
Act swiftly with the
natural flow

Presencing
Retreat and reflect
Allow the inner knowing to emerge

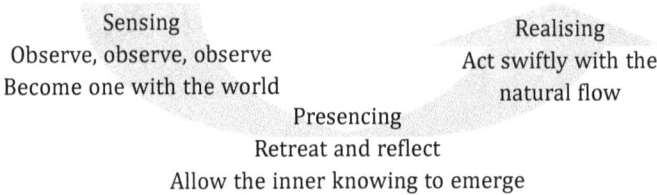

Figure 1: Scharmer's U-Process Model
Source: Adapted from Senge, Scharmer, Jaworski and Flowers (2005:88)

The U-theory suggests co-creation between the individual and the collective, that is, the larger world. It is about the interconnection or integration of the self with the world. At the bottom of the U, as described by Scharmer, is the "inner gate", where we drop the baggage of our journey, and go over a threshold. The metaphor used here is that of "death of the old self" and "rebirth of the new self", and the client emerges with a different sense of self. There is a lovely dialogue between Wilber and Scharmer discussing the seven states and the three movements in this one process (Scharmer, 2003) on the Web.

Superficial learning and change processes are shorter versions of the U-movement. In using this as a coaching process, the client moves downwards into the base of the U, moving from acting, to thinking, to feeling, to will. This is to help the client to download with the coach, to let go and discover who they really are, to see from the deepest part of themselves, developing an awareness that is expanded with a shift in intention.

Otto Scharmer, in an executive summary of his new book *Theory U: Leading from the Future as it Emerges*, describes the U-process as five movements: co-initiating, co-sensing, presencing, co-creating and co-evolving (Scharmer, 2007:5–8). Scharmer describes this as moving, "first into intimate connection with the world and to a place of inner knowing that can emerge from within, followed by bringing forth the new, which entails discovering the future by doing" (Scharmer, 2007).

The following figure and case study demonstrate the five-step process.

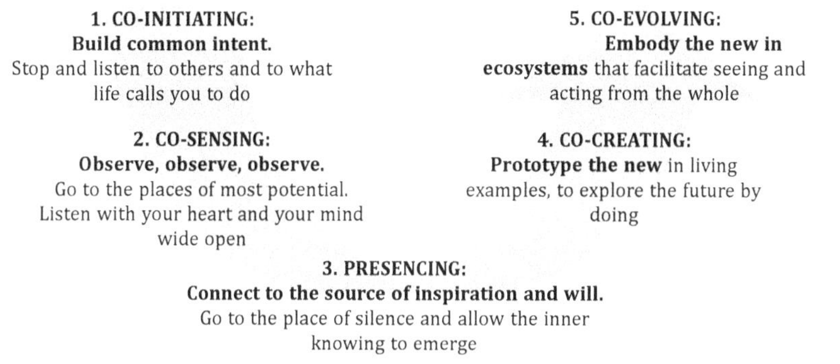

1. CO-INITIATING:
Build common intent.
Stop and listen to others and to what
life calls you to do

5. CO-EVOLVING:
Embody the new in
ecosystems that facilitate seeing and
acting from the whole

2. CO-SENSING:
Observe, observe, observe.
Go to the places of most potential.
Listen with your heart and your mind
wide open

4. CO-CREATING:
Prototype the new in living
examples, to explore the future by
doing

3. PRESENCING:
Connect to the source of inspiration and will.
Go to the place of silence and allow the inner
knowing to emerge

Figure 2: U-process case study
Source: Scharmer (2007:6)

Case study: The Global Convention on Coaching (GCC)

From July 2007 until July 2008, I played a role as Chair of the GCC Working Group, Research Agenda for Development of the Field, and Carol Kauffman took the part of Facilitator. The GCC was originally established to create a collaborative dialogue for all stakeholders in coaching worldwide, with the ultimate aim of professionalising the industry. Nine initial working groups were formed by the GCC's Steering Committee to discuss critical issues related to the professionalisation of coaching, producing "White Papers" on the current realities and possible future scenarios of these issues. These White Papers were presented at the GCC's Dublin Convention in July 2008.

Using the U-process model, this case study summarises the working group process of the research agenda, which comprised a 12-month online dialogue process, with the addition of monthly telephone conversations during 2007–2008. The White Papers for all nine working groups (plus the new tenth group: Coaching and Society) are available at http://www.coachingconvention.org/.

1. **Co-initiation**

   Co-initiating is about building common intent, stopping and listening to others and to what life calls you to do. In the Working Group for the Research Agenda, the group built common intent by setting up the group, defining their purpose, and beginning to discuss the process that they wanted to use for their dialogue. It was agreed that the chair and facilitator would invite specific individuals to join the Working Group, and that those members would suggest other individuals who might have a key interest in the research agenda for the field (namely, the emerging coaching profession). The group began their online dialogue once all had accepted the invitation and received instructions on how to use the online GCC web forum. It was agreed that there would be three communities working together: the Working Group; the Consultative Body for the Research Agenda; and the Steering Committee, who were responsible for the leadership and management of the other groups.

2. **Co-sensing**

   Observe, observe, observe. Go to the places of most potential and listen with your mind and heart wide open. The chair and the facilitator of the Working Group had to learn to co-facilitate, observing each other's skill and competence. They had to be willing to listen to each other, observing each other's style in facilitating and online dialogue. They needed to create the group and facilitate the way forward, learning to take constructive criticism and appreciation from each other. They needed to guide the group forward without being prescriptive. Both chair and facilitator agreed to co-chair the process, remaining mentally and emotionally open to each other's divergent opinions, ways of being, and styles of interpersonal communication, whether working with the group online or by phone.

3. **Presencing**

   Connect to the source of inspiration and will. Go to the place of silence and allow the inner knowing to emerge. Each individual in the process reflected and regularly added their thoughts and feelings to the online forum. Debate, conflict and agreement emerged, with the chair and facilitator taking responsibility for keeping the group on track without being prescriptive. The chair and facilitator had to connect, each one to his or her own individual source of inspiration, and to bring those together as one voice to guide the group.

4. Co-creating

Prototype the new in living examples, to explore the future by doing. This entailed harnessing the energy of the Working Group to draft a current reality document of their online and teleconference dialogues; this document was revised four times. They brought in a facilitator for a second Consultative Body, who entered the Consultative Body dialogue at stage 1 (co-initiating), but who, at the same time, entered the Working Group dialogue at stage 3 (presencing). Trying to move forward with their own Working Group process, yet move the Consultative Body from stage 1 to stage 2 (co-initiation to co-sensing) was a complex parallel process. The chair and facilitator enlisted the help of an editor, Nick Wilkins, to manage the writing process of the White Paper during the Working Group's co-creation (or stage 4).

5. Co-evolving

Embody the new in ecosystems that facilitate seeing and acting from the whole. The final stage of the process was the physical gathering at the Dublin Convention. This took place in three stages: pre-Convention, Convention, and post-Convention (post-Convention work has just begun). Several months prior to the Convention, all nine working groups began to work together online and by telephone to share their own varied stages in the U-process; in this way they learned from each other as they gathered momentum moving towards Dublin, which was to be the culmination of their year-long project. Some groups had lost participants during the 12 months through disagreement; others had managed to harness the energy to move through each of the stages together. The three processes were:

- **Pre-Convention:** Preparation for the presentation of a White Paper by nine committees; this was for their committee's current global reality and future possible scenarios for their topic, with the addition of a tenth committee four months prior to Dublin.

- **Convention:** Physical presence, dialogue and debate in Dublin with each of the working groups. This was paralleled with virtual online feedback on a daily basis from those not able to attend the Convention (however, there were difficulties with this process, which frustrated some who could not access the virtual dialogue during that week).

- **Post-Convention:** Continuation of the process with a new format. The work was to take place in diverse groups regionally and nationwide, to proceed to the next step of building the emerging profession of coaching. Post-Convention, a Transitional Steering Group (TSG) has begun work on harnessing the energy of those wishing to continue. The new GCC sees its role as an organic one, continuing to facilitate a global dialogue, rather than forming another coaching organisation. The GCC Transitional Steering Group (TSG), with representatives from the USA, UK, Australia Argentina, Singapore and South Africa, designed a web-based networking platform for the 17 000 GCC members who had signed up to the *Dublin Declaration on Coaching* (GCC, 2008). (Those who wish to take part in this ongoing worldwide dialogue were able to access it via the web on gccweb.ning. com). Thereafter, preparations were made for the convention in London on 9–10 July 2010.

This U-process is applicable to large innovation projects where the unfolding takes place over a long time; a year in this instance. The team composition in such projects will change and adapt to some degree after each movement. In the GCC process, the working group for the Research

Agenda had lost and added new members, whereas the consultative body was a looser entity with only certain members playing a strong role. This was a process of discovery, exploring the future by doing, thinking and reflecting. As Scharmer explains, it facilitates an opening. Facilitating an opening process involves "the tuning of three instruments: the open mind, the open heart, and the open will" (Scharmer, 2007:8–9).

Conclusion

Models offer a great sense of structure yet flexibility for the coach practitioner, but remember that simplicity is a prerequisite. In this series, I explore models from an experiential learning premise, as the client always brings their experience into the coaching conversation. The client's experience is underpinned by a range of factors, including gender, race, culture, education, life experience and personality. In my next article, we will begin to explore the use of four quadrant models.

References

- Global Convention on Coaching (GCC). 2008g. *Dublin Declaration on Coaching Including Appendices.* Global Convention on Coaching. Dublin, August. Webpage: http://www.coachingconvention.org/.

- Scharmer, O. 2003. Mapping the Integral U: A conversation between Ken Wilber and Otto Scharmer, Denver, CO, 17 September. *Dialog on Leadership.* Webpage: www.dialogonleadership.org/interviews/Wilber.html.

- Scharmer, CO. 2007. *Addressing the Blind Spot of Our Time: An Executive Summary of the New Book by Otto Scharmer: Theory U: Leading from the Future as it Emerges.* Theoryu.com. Webpage: www.theoryu.com/execsummary.html.

- Senge, P, Scharmer, CO, Jaworski, J, and Flowers, B S. 2005. *Presence: Exploring Profound Change in People, Organizations and Society.* London: Nicholas Brealey.

- Stout Rostron, S. 2009. *Business Coaching Wisdom and Practice: Unlocking the Secrets of Business Coaching.* Johannesburg: Knowledge Resources.

❖ ❖ ❖ ❖

How Can I Approach The Human Spirit? The New Coach's Transformation

by David B Drake, Diane Brennan and Kim Gørtz

From: *The Philosophy and Practice of Coaching: Insights and Issues for a New Era.* David B Drake (Editor), Diane Brennan and Kim Gørtz.

David B Drake, PhD, is the Executive Director of the Center for Narrative coaching in California (www.narrativecoaching.com). The Center works with organisations to improve their coaching capabilities and to develop an integrated strategy so that coaching becomes the way business gets done. David teaches advanced narrative/coaching skills around the world, and he works with several universities on coaching development and narrative research. He is a co-founder of the Coaching Commons (www.coachingcommons.org). David has written over twenty articles, papers and chapters on narratives, evidence, and coaching.

Diane Brennan is an executive coach and consultant working with individuals and organisations in the fields of health care, academics and business. She holds a Master's in Business Administration and is acknowledged by the International Coach Federation (ICF) as a Master Certified Coach. Prior to coaching, Diane spent over 20 years in executive and clinical practice positions within private and publicly traded health care organisations in the United States.

Kim Gørtz holds a master degree in philosophy and psychology from the University of Copenhagen. He has taught at the Copenhagen Business School for seven years as well as Roskilde University and the University of Southern Denmark. For the past three years Kim has been conducting an industrial PhD research project for the Nordea Bank, with a focus on coaching, leadership development, and engagement. He has published several books on philosophy in business life, philosophy and coaching, and value-based leadership.

We identify the steps in the process that will help new coaches to move into a more empowering partnership with clients who are ready, willing and able to take responsibility for their own lives and begin the courageous work to move towards living their dreams, visions and purposes.

The New Coach's Transformation

The challenge for most new coaches we train is to make the personal transition from giving advice to letting go of their own agenda in favour of the client's agendas. Most new coaches are quite comfortable giving advice to family, friends and associates about how they "should be" doing something to improve their life/or achieve their goals. In fact, most of them have been sought out for their ability to give such advice. They have become good at it, are proud of supporting their loved ones, and are now seeking to learn a formal structure so they can get paid to do this. The good news is that they care deeply for people's wellbeing. However, they also come to recognise the down-sides of their old ways of "supporting" people, including:

- Most people have not followed their advice – no matter how spectacular it was.

- They have not always been as fully appreciated as they would like to be.

- The same "issues" always seem to come back for people, over and over, without any discernible progress, clarity, commitment, or resolution.

- They have never been compensated for their brilliant advice.

Steps in the Process

The primary aim is to help coaches shift from giving advice to focus on helping the client to know more fully and deeply his own Human Spirit. In training coaches, we have found the following two steps to be essential in helping them move into a more empowering partnership with clients who are ready, willing and able to take responsibility for their own lives and begin the courageous work to move towards living their dreams, visions and purposes.

Step 1: Facilitate each client to get to know his or her unique Human Spirit

My greatest contribution to my coaching client is to facilitate her to get to know her unique Human Spirit.

We have a passion for supporting our new coaches to getting to really know themselves and to training them in such a manner that they in turn can support their coaching clients to really know themselves. This work has to be the first step in establishing the coaching foundation. Without it, the client and coach are wandering in the wilderness and will have difficulty anchoring the client's goals and objectives to his or her Human Spirit. Instead, the client will remain caught in his or her conditioning that more money, the next promotion, or the approval of someone else will bring happiness or satisfaction – the payoff he or she is seeking. However, most of the time these payoffs are anchored to something that is outside of the client and, as a result, the payoffs lack sufficient meaning and personal significance for the client.

Based on our experience, we know that any achievement or payoff that is not directly linked to the person's Human Spirit is, by design, going to leave the person unfulfilled and frustrated in the end. We also know that the continual setting, and even achieving, of goals that are primarily externally driven lead to a loss of motivation and a growing sense of burnout. So if repetition of what the client has already been doing, even if it is with great efficiency, is not the answer, what is? We have found that the answer is to help the to client access (not assess) his or her Human Spirit. We have heard clients also call this soul, true self, essential nature, or God self. We strongly encourage the coach to use and honour the language of the client during the coaching relationship. For the purpose of this article we will refer to it as the "Human Spirit".

How can I do it?

We have identified the following three stages that masterful coaches can use to get to know and reconnect with their Human Spirit.

193

Stage 1

Facilitate the client in a process that will lead to a deeper awareness of herself. We use a model that incorporates four levels at which to work depending on the capability and readiness of the coach and the client.

- *Level 1:* Use assessment tools that employ classification of preferences, for example, relating, communicating, deciding. These can be helpful as a starting point with people who are new to this work – clients who are not ready to do the deeper work and/or coaches who are not trained in the use of techniques to access deeper levels.

- *Level 2:* Use list-making tools (for example, values, purposes, talents) to surface how the client frames, interprets and responds to the world. Working at this level helps the client to make more refined distinctions, particularly between what he or she has adopted from his or her upbringing and environment and what he or she wants to bring forward in his or her life.

- *Level 3:* Ask the client to describe experiences, events and accomplishments that have brought him or her joy. Working at this level helps the client to access memories and emotions that provide glimpses into her Human Spirit and the values, purposes and talents that are present. It is important to help the client to separate behaviours or accomplishments that have been rooted in pleasing others from those that have come from being true to his or her own Human Spirit.

- *Level 4:* Invite the client to relax into a guided visualisation where he or she describes a place in the future or an ideal scene. While in this altered state of consciousness, ask him or her to describe what qualities, accomplishments, talents and passions are being visualised. This level bypasses the client's current ego, reality, limitations, and past assumptions to get what is innately important to and nourishes his or her Human Spirit.

Stage 2

Work with the client to articulate his or her values, life purposes, and his or her unique and natural talents from the deepest level he or she was able to access using the steps above. We have found the greatest success in asking the client questions while in the altered state reached at stage 4. At whatever level the client reaches, the coach writes down those words and phrases from the client that are filled with a passionate energy. We have found in our work that it is helpful to the process if the coach does not describe the process, as a "values clarification", "life purpose" or "talent identification" process because doing so often evokes a more linear, cerebral and predictable response from clients. Instead, masterful coaches position it as a "discovery process" or "foundational process" that is intended to assist the client during his or her coaching relationship. Using a more open term seems to enable greater access, based in the moment and not on pre-formed terms, to the client's Human Spirit.

In order to be effective, the masterful coach has become proficient at:

- Guiding the client to a stage 4 depth of access (as described above)
- Distilling the client's words, phrases and energy into an accurate reflection of what the client has revealed (without consciously knowing it yet) as his or her:
    - Unique set of values
    - Unique life-purpose statement
    - Unique combination of natural strengths and talents.

Stage 3

Invite the client to take the words and phrases written down by the coach and work with them to express them in a fashion that is personally meaningful and generative. Once the client feels complete with the process and his or her articulation of the results, the coach can then share with her the frame and terms for what he or she has developed – core values, life purpose, and strengths/talents.

When these three stages of client discovery are approached in the manner described here, the client is often moved to a humble reverence of who he or she has always known him or herself to be, through being able to articulate it so succinctly, accurately and powerfully. As an example, a recent client wrote at the end of this discovery process:

My core values: Creative, connection, thriving, compassionate, of service.

My life purpose: I am the exquisite and playful orchestration of Spirit's oneness and Human's uniqueness that come together to create a bodacious flourishing of life.

My unique talents: Conceptual, easily articulate the complex, deep listener, patience, trust, visionary, designer, facilitator.

When a client is able to articulate key elements of his or her Human Spirit, the coach can listen for/on behalf of the client's best and brightest self. The coach can also use each of these three elements of his or her Human Spirit as the basis for asking powerful questions, creating plans, designing actions, and making requests of the client for commitments to his or her own forward movement. As a result, the masterful coach no longer has to guess where to anchor the client's decisions and actions. The novice coach is now more able to make the transition from unconsciously giving advice and asking leading questions to consciously assessing the client's articulated Human Spirit for direction, clarity and decisions. For clients, there is quite often a sense of receiving, for the first time in their lives, a clear and personal compass that is empowering and easy to apply in everyday situations and choices.

These three elements of the Human Spirit – values, purpose and talents – become the predominant focal point to which the masterful coach now listens for where the client is or is not aligned. The client is always revealing his or her underlying beliefs and aspirations, or some aspects of he or she decision-making, planning and goal-setting process. The masterful coach can now listen through the client own higher consciousness of him- or herself.

Step 2: Facilitate the client's awareness to choose (or not) alignment with his or her human spirit

My second greatest contribution to my coaching client is to create awareness in her to choose if, when, where and how to live his or her life in alignment with his or her unique Human Spirit.

Once the client's Human Spirit is revealed and articulated, the second step is for the coach to support the client to be aware of:

• whether or how his or her goals, dreams, decisions, plans and action steps are aligned and anchored with his or her Human Spirit, and

• to make new choices accordingly.

When a coach is able to evoke the client's Human Spirit, the client has access to greater clarity of purpose and direction in every part of his or her life.

There are many paths

There are times when the client is aware that a planned action is not fully aligned with his or her own values, purposes or talents – for any number of reasons. In these cases, the coach has done his or her job by bringing the client to this conscious awareness; it is the client's right and privilege "to be or not to be" fully him- or herself. In our experience, when a client has consciously chosen a path that was not fully congruent with what the individual knew and believed his or herself to be, this conscious choice of incongruence has always been the precursor to a significant and fulfilling turning point in a client's life.

When coaching from the perspective of Human Spirit, a coach knows, without reservation, that even this seemingly incongruent (and yes, unanchored) path the client is choosing is the path that will best serve this client at this time. In part, this requires the coach to take a wider view on behalf of the client's path. Perhaps there is a lesson to be learned. Perhaps it is to understand the experiences of those people whom the client is being called to serve. Perhaps it is in the very experience of the struggle of trying to be someone he or she is not. Helping a client to gain awareness of any incongruity or misalignment related to a particular course of action allows him or her to connect his or her incongruity with his or her results – including any undesirable fallout, for example, internal feelings or external reactions. The client can choose to recalibrate his or her way of being and doing – or not. We believe it is the client's sole responsibility to make this choice whether to move into greater alignment with whom she now knows herself to be. *To be or not to be...* continues to be a powerful question the coach has a responsibility to ask and which the client has the right to choose consciously.

The masterful coach facilitates the client to access aspects of him- or herself that have lain in the shadows and remained mostly unexplored until now. Most clients do not know or believe what vast resourcefulness is available to them. There is so much more available to us than most people are able to see and know on their own, owing to a lifetime of being told who they are and what they can and cannot do. The masterful coach is a professionally-trained listener. However, questions remains, such as: What is the coach listening for? What is the coach missing as a result of his or her default listening modality? The type of listening used by the coach changes everything in the coaching relationship.

What is the coach listening for?

Most coaches, consciously or unconsciously, are primarily listening for one of the following:

- What is *impeding* the client from reaching his or her goals and dreams? or

- What is *inspiring* the client's actions, plans and decisions in support of reaching his or her goals and dreams?

The "what-impedes-you?" approach

Based on most new coaches' past experience, training and compensation, they are delighted when a client has some fear, block or challenge into which they can dig. The new coach proceeds with a line of questioning designed to eliminate or at least minimise these impediments to a client achieving his or her goals. However, when coaches listen for limiting beliefs, blocks, fears, tolerations, and so on, that is what they will reflect back to their client. Our experience is that this approach to listening makes for arduous coaching for both the client and the coach. The client is led into the areas of low energy and low confidence and reconnected with an all-too-familiar state of struggle. When the coach then asks, "So now, what do you want to accomplish in this session?" or, "What's the next step for you to move towards your goal?" or, "How can you overcome this obstacle?", the client is in a diminished state of resourcefulness marked by his or her gremlins (protection from getting hurt), critical mind (limiting self-talk), and fears about moving forward. The client's mind is literally shut down to a wider range of possibilities.

Coaches we have observed who continue to utilise this approach are also more likely to interject their ideas, advice, strategies, resources, and so on, to assist the client in moving forward. By doing so, the coach takes over the responsibility for finding the client's answers. The burden of having to move the client forward under this type of coaching process shifts from the client to the coach. As one would expect, this is fraught with all the down-sides of giving advice to friends. The client has not been empowered; he or she has again been told what to do. The client has little or no buy-in; the source of answers is still outside of her. The client has been once again robbed of the experience to learn more about him- or herself and to know that he or she is more resourceful than she has ever given him- or herself credit for.

The "what-inspires-you?" approach

When the coach listens for the client's natural strengths, passions, aspirations, core values and life purpose, these are what the coach has available to reflect back to the client, verify that, that is what the coach has heard him or her say, and ask what he wishes to expand on. A client will still bring up his fears and blocks. The difference is that this approach to coaching moves him or her into his or her most resourceful space with an unlimited mind for solutions to appear.

The masterful coach can use this approach to engage the client in a vibrant celebration of his or her Human Spirit and in a co-creative process of new possibilities. Doing so can be exhilarating for both the coach and the client. The coach's role in this process is to know and hold the client's unique Human Spirit at all times and to start from this place in asking questions of, communicating with and acknowledging the client. When the coach comes from the client's self-articulated Human Spirit, the client cannot dissuade his or her coach that he or she is anything but innately magnificent, resourceful, purposeful and talented. At the same time, the coach accepts and allows the client to be stuck if the client is not prepared, for any reason, to move forward. This honours the client's path of learning and his or her humanness in that moment.

Table 1 depicts the two approaches to enquiry and listening – one that leads to openness and one that often leads to closure in clients. These two approaches are illustrated with common questions at each of the three different levels in terms of what the coach is listening for and seeking to access.

Table 1: Comparison of the two approaches

	The "what-impedes-you?" approach	The "what-inspires-you?" approach
What mindset informs my questioning?	Questions that often result in the client closing down	Questions that often result in the client opening up
What level of access informs my questions?	My-client-is-strictly-human approach: Questions that can restrict or limit the client	My-client-is-a-Human-Spirit approach: Questions that can expand the client
Accessing the client's internal world	• *What fears are you holding back?* • *What are your internal obstacles?*	• *What part of this aligns with your core values, life purposes and natural talents?*

Accessing the clients external world	• What blocks are in your way that you will need to overcome?	• What impact will your vision have on your world?
Accessing the client's system or source of resourcefulness	• What part of your past training or area of expertise can support your quest? • What has made you successful in the past?	• What is that quiet connection to your Human Spirit saying to you now? • What is your inner guidance showing you?

Establishing the client's Human Spirit

All coaches want the best for their client. However, we have found that in working with "what-inspires-you", coaches are less likely to listen to clients through their own autobiographical filters of what may or may not be true for the client. By helping the client to articulate his or her own Human Spirit, coaches have a key to help their clients attain greater fulfilment, satisfaction, peace, love, and an experience of heaven on earth.

❖ ❖ ❖ ❖

Sample of a Generic Mentorship/ Coaching Agreement

Date	
Version Number	
Review Date	
Definitions	
Mentor	

Definitions:

Mentor:

The mentor fulfils the role of trusted counsellor or teacher, and in the context of this agreement, the more experienced person in the pairing. The role includes pairing with the mentee or protégé in order to:

- Facilitate personal and career development and advancement

- Achieve educational advancement (*delete if not applicable)*

- Build and maintain networks.

Mentor's name:

Mentee/protégé:

The mentee or protégé (terms used interchangeably) fulfils the role of learner or student, that is, the one whose development is guided, informed and facilitated by the mentor.

Mentee's name	
Sponsor	

The protégé is sponsored by ....

Line manager: ....

The protégé reports to .... (*name, role title, department*)

Human Resources Contact:

The Human Resources contact responsible for the protégé's file is...............................

Period

Initiation date	
Termination date	

The parties will meet once a *week/month/fortnight* for the duration of the programme. The contract is for a total of .... hours of mentoring time, with each face-to-face meeting being a period of *60/90/120* minutes.

Should either party not be able to attend a scheduled meeting, he or she should notify the other timeously, and immediately arrange an alternative session.

Additional support

In addition to the scheduled face-to-face sessions, the protégé is entitled to one 30-minute telephonic session per month, at his or her cost. This should be scheduled in advance between the two parties, and can be initiated by either mentor or protégé, depending on necessity.

The mentor will supply the protégé with .... articles or reading material (URLs for relevant websites, abstracts, book chapters or summaries, etcetera) each month. These will be emailed to the protégé, who is expected to read them before the next scheduled session.

The mentor has set up a blog to which all protégés have access. The URL for the blog is ....

The protégé is encouraged to read postings, but is not required to make comments or add posting, although this is encouraged in order to share experiences with others.

Time out

Because of the seasonal nature of the protégé's role, he or she will not be required to engage in face-to-face sessions between .... and .... During this time, he or she is encouraged to utilise the telephonic support facility, and read and participate in the mentor's blog. The mentor will continue to supply regular articles, which the protégé is required to read.

In the event of any of the following arising, the mentor and protégé will agree on an appropriate period during which all active mentoring will cease and when it will recommence. These details will be incorporated into Version ... of this agreement.

- Pregnancy

- Sabbaticals

- Long leave

- Formal training or studies.

Goals and content

(These should be drawn from the personal requirements of the person to be mentored, and aligned with the architecture.)

List the goals very specifically, preferably in table form, with due dates and measures.

Goal	Due date	Measure

Learning objective	Associated behaviour	Associated long-term development need	Associated short-term development need	Due date

Responsibility charter

We, the mentor and mentee, agree, by our signatures hereto, and commit ourselves to the best of our ability to:

- Be physically and psychologically present for each other during interactions

- Abide by the terms of the agreement

- Prepare before each session

- Engage in constructive dialogue and discussion

- Follow advice or recommendations that might be sought

- Engage in facilitating a mutual learning experience.

I, the sponsor, as representative of .... (*organisation name*) agree, by my signature hereto, to commit myself and .... (*organisation name*) to the best of our ability to:

- Make it possible for both parties to participate fully in the programme

- Measure, monitor and review progress and create opportunities for regular feedback to mentor, mentee and other appropriate stakeholders

- Provide an environment supportive of the mentoring or coaching programme.

Signatures:
Mentor
Protégé
Sponsor

❖ ❖ ❖ ❖

INDEX

www.ingramcontent.com/pod-product-compliance
Lightning Source LLC
Chambersburg PA
CBHW070514200326
41519CB00013B/2800